Happy, Healthy Houseplants

How to Stop Loving Your Plants to an Early Grave

Kellyn Kennerly

Creator of Easy Growing

PAGE STREET
PUBLISHING CO.

PAGE STREET
PUBLISHING CO.

Copyright © 2024 Kellyn Kennerly

First published in 2024 by
Page Street Publishing Co.
27 Congress Street, Suite 1511
Salem, MA 01970
www.pagestreetpublishing.com

Distributed by Macmillan, sales in Canada by The Canadian Manda Group.

28 27 26 25 24   1 2 3 4 5

ISBN-13: 979-8-89003-142-6

Library of Congress Control Number: 2023949743

Edited by Sadie Hofmeester
Cover and book design by Caitlyn Boyd for Page Street Publishing Co.
Photography and photography research by Kellyn Kennerly, except for select stock images
(see page 188 for full list)

Printed and bound in China

Page Street Publishing protects our planet by donating to nonprofits like The Trustees, which focuses on local land conservation.

To my husband, Dalton, and my mother, Michelle, for always believing in me, even when I couldn't believe in myself. I love you both endlessly.

Contents

The Houseplant Revolution

In the midst of digital overload and the rapid pace of the 21st century, a hopeful trend has taken root. A green revival has popped up within apartment buildings and suburban homes alike. Houseplants, once mere backdrops, have emerged as symbols of reconnecting with nature and rediscovering the joy of nurturing amidst a world that often feels disconnected and chaotic.

During the unsettling times of 2020, as the world grappled with a pandemic, my own internal struggles with anxiety and depression found solace in these living beings. My home, initially a sanctuary-turned-prison during the COVID-19 lockdown, slowly blossomed into an indoor jungle. The classic *Monstera deliciosa*, my first plant, marked the beginning of this green journey and offered a beacon of hope amidst despair. Each morning, replacing the habitual dive into the abyss of thoughts or social media, I found peace in the routine of checking the moisture levels of the soil and eagerly awaiting new growth.

My story isn't singular. This resurgence of interest in houseplants isn't just a decorative pursuit; it reflects our innate desire for tranquility and our craving to nurture. During lockdown, as we became trapped in concrete jungles and our worlds shrunk smaller and smaller, the act of caring for these plants became a therapeutic ritual for many. For me, it was transformative, turning my 1,300 square foot living space into a testament of resilience and growth. Houseplants became not just a part of my daily routine, but integral to my mental well-being.

Research from Indiana University has shown that tending to plants can have a profound effect on mental health, alleviating symptoms of anxiety and depression. In my experience, this isn't just a statistic reality but a lived one. Plants taught me the value of patience, the importance of routine and the beauty of life's many forms through life and death.

In this book, we'll explore twenty popular houseplants that have captivated the hearts of modern enthusiasts. We'll delve into their histories, care secrets and the unique charm that makes them loved in homes worldwide. We will also take a dive into a guide (created from firsthand experience!) for the anxious plant parent, as well as five DIY projects to spice up your houseplant hobby. This book, crafted for both the experienced and the novice, aims to enlighten and inspire by cultivating a deeper connection with these pieces of nature living in our homes.

As we embark on this journey, remember the lessons these plants teach us about the patience, resilience and simple joy of watching life unfold. So, take a deep breath and feel the fresh oxygen courtesy of our leafy friends. Join me in the lush world of houseplants. They are more than just décor; they are life companions that have seen many of us at our lowest and been instrumental in our journeys toward healthier minds. In their silent companionship, they remind us that growth, even under the direst circumstances, is not only possible but inevitable.

Kellyn Kennerly

Understanding Plant Basics

In this chapter, we will explore six key areas to help you create the ideal environment for your houseplants: light, water, soil, climate, fertilization and common issues. From the humidity-loving aroids to the sun-basking succulents, you'll learn how to create the ideal environments for these plants in your own space. We'll also touch upon the essentials of plant care, from watering techniques to light requirements, ensuring that you have all the tools necessary to nurture and grow your indoor jungle.

The Role of Light

What Is Direct, Indirect and Low Light?

Nature's infinite wisdom has crafted plants to be attuned to their environment, responding to the changing seasons and the shifting sun. Light, an essential yet often misunderstood component, plays a pivotal role in the health, vitality and aesthetic appeal of the plants we keep in our homes. I can confidently say that light is the number one aspect of plant care you must get right in order for your indoor plants to thrive year-round. It influences not just their growth, but also their ability to flower, produce new leaves and remain vigorous amidst the varying conditions of any indoor environment.

Because my current home doesn't receive a lot of natural lighting, I supplement with various artificial grow lights (page 16). If you choose to supplement with grow lights, you will want to invest in modern, full-spectrum lights that are designed to mimic sunlight's spectrum. Investing in grow lights is especially important during the winter months when most spaces receive less natural lighting. In today's world, with the recent surge in houseplant popularity, there are many grow lights on the market to choose from that are not only effective but also aesthetically pleasing.

Direct Light

When we speak of direct light in the context of houseplants, we refer to sunlight that reaches the plant without any obstruction. The rays do not pass through curtains, shades or any semitransparent material. It is the bold, unfiltered sunlight that bathes the plant in a bright and powerful glow—sometimes more powerful than the plant's liking. Plants that typically thrive in direct light are often those that originate from environments where the sun blazes down upon the landscape, such as cacti (page 137), succulents (page 141) and some tropical species.

You can acclimate some tropicals to withstand direct light by slowly adjusting the amount they receive each day until they have adapted to tolerate harsh, direct lighting. They will develop mechanisms, like thick, fleshy leaves or a particular leaf orientation, to absorb and store water, manage intense light and protect against desiccation. Desiccation in houseplants, essentially their dehydration, manifests through several distinct signs. The most obvious is the presence of dry, crispy leaves that often turn brown at the tips or edges. These leaves might appear shriveled or wilted, indicating a severe lack of moisture. In more advanced stages, the plant's soil will be extremely dry, and you may notice the leaves dropping off. Some tropicals that can withstand direct light, if introduced properly, include hoya (page 111), ficus (page 85) and alocasia (page 65).

Indirect Light

Indirect light is a good call for any plant, especially if you are unsure of its wants and needs in the beginning of your relationship.

Bright, indirect light is a key lighting condition for houseplants, where sunlight is softened before reaching the plant. This often happens through sheer curtains or light reflection from walls. Plants in such light enjoy a well-lit but not harsh environment, mimicking the conditions of forest clearings. It's ideal for plants needing more light without the risk of leaf burn. Bright, indirect light enhances the growth and color of many houseplants, especially variegated or brightly colored ones, making it a great choice for uncertain lighting conditions.

Medium, indirect light is a gentler and less intense form of lighting, found farther inside a room or near north-facing windows. It resembles the dappled sunlight of dense forest canopies. Plants suited for this light are typically from lower forest layers, thriving in consistent but muted brightness. Medium, indirect light supports steady growth in plants that require less intense conditions, making them suitable for areas with limited natural light.

Low Light

Low light should not be mistaken for no light. Low-light areas are notably less bright than spots with direct or indirect light. These might be areas that are farther from windows or in rooms that receive minimal natural light. Low-light conditions can still support a variety of houseplants, particularly those that are naturally adapted to the shaded forest floor, such as the ZZ plant or the snake plant (page 129). These plants have developed strategies to survive (and even thrive) in less illuminated environments, maximizing whatever light is available to sustain their growth.

As previously stated, low light does not mean no light! All plants require some amount of light to photosynthesize. If you would like to add some greenery to your dimly lit bathroom or basement, perhaps consider supplementing with grow lights (page 16).

Window Placement and Sunlight

Understanding the orientation of windows in your home is crucial for providing the right light conditions for houseplants. North-, south-, east- and west-facing windows each offer different qualities and intensities of sunlight, affecting how plants grow.

North-facing windows receive the least amount of direct sunlight. The light through these windows is generally cool and diffused, making them ideal for plants that thrive in low to medium light. However, light-loving plants might not receive enough sunlight in this orientation.

South-facing windows are the most sun-drenched, receiving the most intense and longest duration of light throughout the day. This bright exposure is perfect for sun-loving plants. Caution is advised during summer months, as the intense light can sometimes be too harsh for certain plants.

East-facing windows offer bright morning sunlight, which is gentler compared to the harsh midday sun. This makes them suitable for plants that appreciate bright but not overly intense light, such as orchids (page 101) or philodendrons (page 55). Plants placed in an east-facing window will enjoy the morning sunshine without the risk of scorching.

West-facing windows receive strong afternoon and evening sun, which can be quite intense during the hotter parts of the year. This sunlight is more potent than the gentle morning rays coming through east-facing windows but slightly less harsh than the midday sun typical of south-facing exposures. The light from west-facing windows can be particularly strong during the late afternoon, making these windows an excellent spot for plants that enjoy a good dose of sunshine but may not require all-day exposure.

Each window orientation offers a unique light environment, and understanding these differences can help you place your plants in the most beneficial spots. By matching plant species with their preferred light conditions, you can ensure healthier growth and more vibrant plant life in your indoor garden.

Artificial Grow Lights

Artificial grow lights are essential for indoor gardening, particularly in areas with limited natural sunlight or during seasons with shorter days.

When selecting grow lights, it's important to consider the light spectrum. Full-spectrum lights are the most effective, as they emulate natural sunlight and provide a balance of cool and warm wavelengths. The intensity of the light should match the needs of your plants, with high-light plants like succulents (page 141) requiring more intensity than low-light varieties such as ferns (page 71). There are various types of grow lights available, including energy-efficient LEDs suitable for most plants; fluorescent lights ideal for seedlings and low-light plants; and high-intensity HID lights for larger plants. Size and placement of your grow lights also play a crucial role; the lights should cover your plant area adequately and be positioned at a distance that benefits the plants without causing heat damage.

The duration of light exposure is typically around 12 to 16 hours per day for most houseplants, though seedlings may thrive with 16 to 18 hours. Observing your plants' response to the lighting is important; signs of distress like legginess or leaf burn may indicate the need for adjustments. Maintaining a consistent light schedule using a timer can help mimic natural day and night cycles, which is beneficial for plant health. Additionally, consider the heat emission of the grow lights to ensure it aligns with your plants' needs, room conditions and energy efficiency, especially if the lights will be on for long periods. Budget is also a factor, as grow lights vary in price. It's important to find a balance between cost and the specific requirements of your plants. By carefully selecting and using grow lights, you can significantly enhance the growth and vitality of your indoor jungle!

Understanding and harnessing the power of light when caring for houseplants involves recognizing the subtle yet distinct differences in lighting conditions. The symphony of life that plays out in lush foliage is a dance much choreographed by light. By illuminating their world with thoughtful intention, we pave the way for our houseplants to thrive. I hope this section helps shed light on guiding you to curate a thriving, well-lit indoor jungle.

Fun Fact: *Plants exhibit a remarkable phenomenon called photo-tropism, where they actively move their leaves toward the light source to optimize their exposure for efficient photosynthesis.*

Quenching Thirst

When to Water and How

Water is the life force of all living things. It is essential to keep ourselves hydrated, and our houseplants crave the same nourishing liquid. It is a medium through which we communicate care and nurture of shared vitality with our houseplants. The act of watering, to me, feels like an act of self-care. You are providing your plants with the life force they need in order for them to give you the foliage that graces your home with a green, whimsical appeal.

Understanding Plant Thirst

Each plant genus, with their varying places of origin and personal preferences, has some pretty specific watering needs. Some have evolved to hoard water in drier environments, while others have adapted to the consistently damp conditions of tropical forests. Our role, as their keepers in our homes, is to decode their patterns that echo their inherent desires. The most popular houseplants tend to fall into one of two categories: succulents and tropicals.

The Succulent's Sip: For desert-dwelling plants like succulents (page 141) and cacti (page 137), water is a precious, sporadically available resource. To mimic their original environments, it is best to let their soil dry out completely in-between waterings. Once the soil is fully dry, drench the plant in water. Drenching the plant can be done by top or bottom watering (page 20). The goal is to let these plants drink deeply but infrequently, while ensuring the soil is fully soaked when we do water.

The Tropical Drink: In contrast to succulents, tropical plants and aroids like pothos (page 51) or philodendrons (page 55) are accustomed to the frequent rains of their native habitats and prefer consistently moist (not soggy) soil. Their thirst is regular but moderate. I like to let the top 1 to 2 inches (2.5 to 5 cm) of soil dry before allowing them their next drink. It is important to give your tropical houseplants a chunky, aerated soil so that the roots can breathe. A chunky soil will also help prevent root rot (page 34)!

What Kind of Water

While rainwater or distilled water is generally considered the gold standard for our houseplants, tap water is a more accessible option for many. However, it often contains chlorine and, in some areas, fluoride, which can be detrimental to sensitive plants over time. This doesn't mean it's completely off the table! To make tap water safer for plants, let it sit in an open container for about 24 hours before use. This step allows chlorine to evaporate, reducing its concentration. If your tap water is hard, meaning high in minerals like calcium and magnesium, consider using distilled or filtered water occasionally to prevent mineral buildup in the soil.

Keep in mind the temperature of the water; room-temperature water is preferable, as cold water can shock plant roots, particularly in tropical varieties.

When to Water

While generalized rules provide a solid baseline to follow, the true essence of watering wisdom lies in attentiveness and the observation of your plant. The subtle droop or curl of a leaf, the slight wilting or the change in leaf color will let you in on the secrets of the plant's hydration needs. Below you will find three easy ways to know when your plant needs a drink.

Feel the Soil: Dig your finger into the soil up to the second knuckle. In small pots, the soil dries out faster, and the finger test can accurately assess the overall moisture level. However, in larger pots, the surface soil may be dry while deeper soil remains moist. For larger pots, it's better to insert your finger deeper into the soil. You can also use a chopstick for this task. If the chopstick comes out dry, it is likely time to water. If there is soil stuck to the stick, it likely has sufficient water for a while longer. Moisture meters can provide some insight, but personally, I have found the other methods mentioned to be more reliable. Your finger or a chopstick will never fail you!

Note that the finger test is generally more effective for smaller or shallow-rooted plants where the root zone is closer to the surface. However, inspecting your soil regularly is a great habit to get into regardless of what type of plant you have. It can help you spot potential pests (page 32) or determine if it might be time for a repot (page 157).

Observe the Foliage: Watch for any signs of curling, drooping, yellowing or browning, which might indicate over-watering or under-watering. If your leaves are discolored, curling or drooping but the soil is still very wet, this could be a sign of problems lying underneath with the root system. However, if the foliage is discolored, curling or drooping and the soil feels dry, give your plant a drink! It will likely perk back up or uncurl within a few hours. If you are experiencing yellowing or browning on the leaves, you can trim these back as they will not recover. This will give your plants a more polished look.

Check the Weight: One of the easiest ways to check if your plant needs hydrating is to simply lift the pot. A light pot may indicate dry soil, while a heavy one suggests adequate moisture.

Bottom Watering

Bottom watering is a method in which water is absorbed by the plant's roots from the bottom up. Rather than pouring water onto the soil's surface, the plant pot is set in a container of water, allowing the soil to wick up moisture through drainage holes until it's adequately saturated. Over time (about 30 minutes) the plant roots absorb this moisture, ensuring deep hydration. You should only let your plants sit in the water for 30 minutes maximum, because any time longer could oversaturate the root system.

Bottom watering is my preferred method (the majority of the time) for a few different reasons. It ensures deep hydration so your plant is fully content. It prevents moisture-loving pests (like fungus gnats) from making the top inch (2.5 cm) of soil their homes. It prevents over-watering as your plant will only soak up the amount of water that it needs to continue giving you beautiful foliage.

Top Watering

For larger plants, bottom watering may not be an option. When top watering, water the top of the soil, ensuring even and complete soaking. You'll know your plant has enough water once the pot feels heavy and the soil is evenly moist. This is where proper drainage comes into play! Allow the excess water to drain from the bottom of the pot.

Top watering has its benefits as well. It's the easiest way to provide your plant with hydration. It flushes out excess minerals and salts from the soil, which will prevent potential toxicity to the plant. It also provides immediate relief for plants that have dried out considerably.

While both of these methods are fine for your plants, I prefer to alternate the two so the soil can be flushed. Flushing the soil during top watering means pouring enough water over the soil until it runs out of the drainage holes. This process removes excess salts and minerals that accumulate from fertilizers and tap water, helping to maintain a healthy soil environment for the plant. It's important to let the excess water drain out completely to avoid root rot. This practice should be done periodically to keep the soil in good condition. I will bottom water three times and then flush out the soil by top watering the fourth time. This schedule has kept my plants happy for many years.

Misting

Oh, the controversy! Misting is such a hot topic on the internet among plant enthusiasts. While some write it off completely, there are a few benefits to misting your humidity-loving plants.

For plants like ferns (page 71), a gentle misting can supplement their hydration by replicating the moist air of a tropical forest. However, you will have to mist three to four times a day to see any significant benefits. It is best to add a humidifier rather than misting your plants individually, as keeping up with three to four times a day can become a hassle. You can also add a pebble tray filled with water beneath or near your plant to raise the moisture levels in the air nearby.

Seasonal Adjustments

Seasonal changes significantly impact the watering needs of houseplants. During the growing season, typically spring and summer, plants often require more water due to increased light and temperature. An increase of both will stimulate growth and increase evaporation. Conversely, in fall and winter, as most plants enter a dormant phase with lower light levels and cooler temperatures, their water requirements decrease. It's crucial to adjust your watering routine accordingly; water more frequently in the warmer months when the topsoil dries out quickly, and reduce watering in the cooler months, allowing the soil to remain dry for longer between waterings. Over-watering during dormant periods can lead to root rot and other issues, as plants use less water. Always check the soil moisture before watering and remember that the specific needs can vary depending on the plant type and your home environment.

Understanding your plants' watering needs is tuning in to their love language. If you can find the happy medium and harmonious balance of when and how to water your houseplants, you will undoubtedly win them over for years to come.

Soil Science

Choosing the Right Soil for Different Plants

If you want thriving houseplants, it all starts with what's hugging their intricate root systems: the soil. It's more than just dirt; it's a thoughtful mixture of different substrates, which are the very foundation upon which our beloved houseplants anchor their existence. The soil is your plant's home and should be adjusted to its unique and individual needs. The growing medium we keep our plants in plays a pivotal role in ensuring longevity and vibrant foliage.

Why Soil Matters

Before diving in to how to choose the right soil mix, it's essential to grasp why it's crucial to understand what kind of soil your plant is craving. The soil provides plants with:

Anchorage: The soil you choose will be the medium for roots to grow and establish. The root system is like the heartbeat of your plant. The roots anchor and support your plants growth—if they aren't happy, the foliage won't be happy either.

Nutrition: The best potting mix contains essential minerals and nutrients necessary for growth. This is available through worm castings, compost, mycorrhizae, slow-release fertilizer, etc.

Aeration: Spaces within the soil allow roots to access oxygen. This is extremely important for preventing root rot (page 34). The roots need to breathe!

Moisture: Your soil should retain water so it never dries out too quickly or stays saturated for too long. There is a perfect middle ground—a sweet soil spot, if you will.

When you first buy a plant from a nursery or big box store, it is usually in a generic potting mix that isn't specific to the individual plant's needs. Repotting plants into a tailored soil mix after purchasing them from a nursery is crucial for several reasons.

Nursery soil mixes are generally designed for short-term sustainability and may not suit the long-term needs of specific plants regarding drainage, nutrient content and pH balance. Fresh soil ensures better aeration and drainage, essential for healthy root development. It also provides the opportunity to inspect and address any root crowding or health issues.

Additionally, nursery soil can become compacted over time, reducing its effectiveness, and may also be depleted of nutrients or harbor pests and diseases. By repotting into a new, plant-specific mix, you can significantly enhance the plant's growth environment, replenish essential nutrients and mitigate the risk of pests and diseases, ensuring a healthier growth trajectory for your plant.

Components of a Good Potting Mix

My personal houseplant mix is often a blend of several components, each serving a distinct purpose:

Peat Moss or Coco Coir: These organic materials retain moisture while providing a light and airy structure for the root system.

Perlite or LECA: Perlite is a volcanic glass that expands when heated, making it lightweight and porous. LECA, or Lightweight Expanded Clay Aggregate, is a porous ceramic material formed by heating clay in a kiln, resulting in lightweight, round pellets used in construction for insulation and as a soilless growing medium in horticulture.

Both are great amendments to aid with aeration and drainage, ensuring roots don't remain water-logged.

Orchid Bark: Orchid bark will provide your soil with aeration so that the roots can breathe while also providing a bit of minerals to the plant. However, this cannot be the primary means of fertilizing.

Worm Castings: A fantastic source of slow-release nutrients, worm castings are the by-product of earthworm digestion.

Compost: Compost is a nutrient-rich, organic amendment made from decomposed plant material, which enhances soil structure, fertility and microbial activity.

Sand: Sand improves drainage, especially vital for cacti and succulents. I typically leave this ingredient out for tropical mixes.

Choosing the Right Soil for Your Houseplant

The diverse world of houseplants, each with its unique origin and needs, demands different soil types:

For Succulents and Cacti: These desert dwellers crave quick-draining soil. Look for mixes labeled specifically for cacti and succulents, usually rich in sand and perlite.

For Tropical Plants and Aroids: Plants like pothos (page 51) or philodendron (page 55), which hail from rainforests, require soil that's moisture-retentive yet well-draining. A general-purpose potting mix typically retains too much water for these chunky soil lovers. You can enhance its structure with amendments such as orchid bark, perlite or LECA to improve aeration and drainage.

For Orchids: These tree-hugging bloomers need exceptional aeration for their roots. Orchid mixes, typically made up of large chunks of bark, charcoal and sometimes perlite, cater to these needs.

For African Violets: These delicate beauties prefer a slightly acidic soil that's light and porous. Specialized African violet mixes are available, often containing peat moss, perlite and vermiculite.

For Palms: Palms, with their extensive root systems, need a well-aerated soil rich in organic matter. Consider a palm-specific mix or enhance a general potting mix with extra sand and worm castings.

For Ferns: Ferns prefer a loose and loamy soil that drains well. Loamy soil is made up of clay, sand and silt with deposits of humus (decomposed organic matter); rich and fertile, loamy soil helps support these delicate forest dwellers.

Customizing Your Mix

While pre-made potting mixes are convenient, the beauty of houseplant care lies in adaptability and being willing to DIY things on the fly. Feel free to tweak the soil you purchase based on your plant's specific needs and your local environment. If you find a mix retains too much water, add more perlite. If it dries out too quickly, integrate more peat moss or coco coir.

My personal mix for aroids, which encompass about 80% of my collection, includes 40% coco coir, 20% perlite, 20% orchid bark, 15% LECA and 5% worm castings. This mix is extra chunky, and my tropical plants swear by it!

All happy houseplants start with a happy growing medium. By investing in the right soil, we don't just nurture our plants, we mimic how they would be growing in the natural world, ensuring our indoor green sanctuaries not just survive, but truly thrive. Remember, as with all things in nature, it's about harmony. The right soil sets the tune for your lifelong journey with houseplants.

Climate Inside Your Home

Humidity and Temperature

The climate inside of our homes profoundly influences the well-being of our houseplants. Indoor conditions tend to be more stable, with controlled temperatures and lower humidity levels compared to the outdoors. This controlled climate lacks the natural fluctuations and seasonal changes to which many plants have adapted. As a result, houseplants might not experience the cues for natural growth cycles like dormancy or flowering that they would outdoors. Additionally, the typically lower humidity indoors can be challenging for tropical plants, which thrive in more humid environments. You can look at climate as the invisible force of life guiding your plants to act in the ways they do. Understanding the climate inside our homes, its components and fluctuations, is incredibly important to crafting an environment where houseplants can truly live their best lives.

Temperature: The Warmth Quotient

Most houseplants originate from tropical or subtropical regions, and thus, they prefer temperatures ranging from 60 to 75°F (15 to 24°C) during the day. However, a slight drop at night often benefits them.

Sudden temperature fluctuations, especially cold drafts or overheating, can stress plants, leading to leaf drop, wilting or slowed growth. Position plants away from direct heat sources like radiators or cold spots like drafty windows. Consider using a digital thermometer to keep an eye on room temperatures.

Humidity: Moisture in the Air

Indoor humidity refers to the concentration of water vapor present in the air. While we might not always notice it, plants certainly do! Low humidity can cause brown leaf tips, slowed growth or increased susceptibility to pests. Conversely, high humidity without proper airflow can promote fungal diseases.

To raise humidity, you can use a humidifier, place a pebble tray filled with water nearby or group plants together. For lowering humidity, consider using a dehumidifier or improving ventilation by adding a fan nearby.

Air Circulation: A Breath of Fresh Air

Stagnant air can become a breeding ground for pests and diseases. Good air circulation ensures that plants receive fresh carbon dioxide for photosynthesis and helps in preventing moisture-related issues. Poor air circulation can lead to fungal diseases, mold growth and heightened pest issues like spider mites.

You can periodically open windows or use oscillating fans to improve circulation. I leave a few fans running on low 24 hours a day, especially in my grow cabinets. This will help keep your plants happy, especially in high humidity areas.

Seasonal Changes: Transitioning Through the Year

The changing seasons outside influence the indoor climate, especially in regions with pronounced seasonal variations. As heating systems kick in during winters and air conditioners during summers, the indoor environment shifts.

The drier air in winter can stress tropical plants, while the heightened humidity in summer might favor some but distress others. Adjust care routines with the seasons. For instance, consider misting or grouping plants together in winter to counteract low humidity.

Indoor climate is a mosaic of factors, each intertwined and influential. While it might seem daunting at first, recognizing and adjusting to these elements can significantly elevate your houseplant collecting experience. Once you understand the climate that each plant prefers, keeping them happy will be a breeze!

Feeding Time
Basics of Fertilization

Fertilizing your plants might seem intimidating, but at its core, it's all about supplying your plants with the nutrients they need. Plants, like all living beings, require sustenance. All houseplant fertilizers should contain three macronutrients: nitrogen (for healthy leaf and stem growth), phosphorus (for strong root systems, flowers and fruits) and potassium (for various physiological processes and overall plant health).

Why Fertilize?

Fertilizing houseplants is essential because, over time, plants deplete the nutrients available in their soil (if there were any in the soil to begin with). Fertilization replenishes these vital nutrients, ensuring plants have the necessary elements for growth, overall health and resistance to stress. Without regular fertilization, houseplants may exhibit stunted growth, dull foliage and reduced flowering or fruiting.

What is Fertilizer Made Of?

Houseplant fertilizers are composed of a blend of essential nutrients, each playing an important role in plant health and growth. The primary components are:

Nitrogen (N): Promoting healthy leaf and stem growth, nitrogen contributes to the green lushness of the plant. It also contributes to the development of amino acids, the building blocks of proteins, which are vital for cell growth and repair.

Phosphorus (P): Essential for root development, flowering and fruiting, phosphorus supports energy transfer within the plant.

Potassium (K): Crucial for overall plant health, potassium aids in water uptake, enzyme activation and resistance to diseases.

Alongside these macronutrients, houseplant fertilizers also contain micronutrients like calcium, magnesium, iron and manganese, which are needed in smaller quantities but are equally essential for plant growth and development. These nutrients support various physiological functions, from photosynthesis to cell wall strength. Some fertilizers also include beneficial soil amendments like humic acids or beneficial microbes to enhance soil quality and plant health. The specific formulation of a houseplant fertilizer can vary, but the objective is always to provide a balanced diet that supports the diverse needs of indoor plants.

The best NPK (nitrogen-phosphorus-potassium) ratio for general houseplant fertilizer often falls within a balanced formula, typically around 20-20-20 or 10-10-10. This balanced ratio provides equal parts of each primary nutrient, which is suitable for a wide range of houseplants. You will typically see the ratio listed on the front of the fertilizer bottle:

20-20-20 Fertilizer: With 20% nitrogen, 20% phosphorus and 20% potassium, this formula is concentrated. It delivers more nutrients per unit of weight than a less concentrated formula.

10-10-10 Fertilizer: This contains 10% of each nutrient. It's less concentrated, meaning it provides fewer nutrients per unit of weight compared to 20-20-20.

When using 20-20-20, less product is needed to deliver the same amount of nutrients that a larger amount of 10-10-10 would provide. Thus, the choice between them can depend on the specific nutritional needs of your plants and how frequently you wish to apply fertilizer.

However, it's also important to note that specific plants may have unique needs. For instance, flowering plants might benefit from a higher phosphorus content, while foliage plants might prefer a nitrogen-rich formula. Always consider the specific needs of your plants but, when in doubt, a balanced, all-purpose houseplant fertilizer is usually a safe choice.

Types of Fertilizers: Liquid vs. Slow Release

Liquid Fertilizer: This is a water-soluble fertilizer, typically available in concentrate form. It's diluted with water and applied directly to the plant's soil or foliage. I personally prefer to use liquid fertilizer over slow-release fertilizer. It seems to give you a bit more control over the nutrients your plant is or isn't receiving.

Since it's in a soluble form, plants can quickly absorb the nutrients. Liquid fertilizer also allows for frequent and controlled feedings, catering to specific plant needs. My favorite advantage of liquid fertilizers is that some can be used as both a root drench and a foliar spray! This means that not only will the soil soak in the benefits, but you can also physically spray your foliage to fertilize the plant as well.

Fun Fact: Foliar feeding, where a diluted nutrient solution is sprayed onto the leaves, can provide rapid absorption of vital nutrients. This is especially helpful when a quick remedy is needed for nutrient deficiencies.

Slow-Release Fertilizer: Often in pellet or granular form, this type of fertilizer gradually releases nutrients over an extended period when watered. Slow-release fertilizer is typically added to the soil mix. You can do this by mixing it in and then potting your plant up or by sprinkling it on top of the soil and working it in. A single application can feed plants for several months.

Slow release is considered a low maintenance form of plant care, which would be an ideal approach for caretakers who prefer a "set it and forget it" approach. This method provides a steady nutrient supply, reducing the risk of burning foliage. The only con to slow-release fertilizer is that you can't stop the food intake, even when your plant is leaving its growing season or going dormant. Fertilizing plants during their dormant season can be harmful as their reduced metabolic activity leads to unused nutrients accumulating in the soil. This can cause nutrient burn, root damage and weak, unsustainable growth. You would need to repot the plant into fresh potting soil without added fertilizer if you ever intended on lessening its diet.

How to Choose?

The choice between liquid and slow-release fertilizers depends on various factors:

Plant Type: Some plants, especially fast growers, might benefit from the immediate boost of liquid fertilizers. Slow growers or established plants might do well with a consistent, slow-release feed.

Gardener's Schedule: Those who enjoy frequent interactions with their plants might prefer liquid fertilizers. On the other hand, individuals with busy schedules or many plants might opt for the convenience of slow-release formulations.

Specific Needs: If a plant shows signs of a nutrient deficiency, a quick-acting liquid fertilizer can help address the issue promptly. For general maintenance, a slow-release option might suffice.

Whichever you choose, always follow the directions on your specific fertilizer to avoid overfertilization.

Fertilization isn't just about feeding; it's about understanding and catering to a plant's evolving needs. Whether you choose the swift action of liquid fertilizers or the slow release of granular options, the goal remains the same: ensuring your plants have a well-rounded diet that propels them toward their fullest potential. Remember, a well-fed plant is often a happy, flourishing one.

The Common Issues

When and How to Intervene

Houseplants, while generally resilient, aren't immune to challenges. As with all living things, they have specific needs, and when those aren't met, problems arise. Recognizing these issues and understanding when and how to act is crucial. I treat almost all of my plants identically if they are facing the same issues. Let's explore some of the most common challenges faced by houseplant lovers and provide insights on timely interventions. For more specific diagnostics concerning individual plants, flip to the plant you are dealing with and read the "Common Problems and Solutions" section.

Yellowing Leaves

Cause: Yellowing leaves often serve as a distress signal and could point to a few different issues, the most common of which are over-watering, frequent dry periods or simply aged foliage.

Intervention: As with all plants, over-watering can cause root rot (page 34). This is the most common road taken to yellowed leaves. To mitigate this, provide your plant with a well-draining soil mix and be sure that you are letting the top 2 inches (5 cm) of soil dry between waterings.

In the same breath, inconsistent watering can also stress your plant, causing a similar yellowing response. Be sure you aren't watering too often or leaving a long gap in between waterings.

Finally, age is something neither we nor the plants can escape. Aged, yellowing leaves will typically show up at the bottom of your plant, closest to the soil. This is part of the plant life cycle and is completely normal. I personally trim these leaves off to redirect energy toward the healthier foliage and new emerging growth.

Drooping or Wilting

Cause: While typically a sign of under-watering, over-watering can also be the culprit when it comes to lifeless leaves. Root rot (page 34) or a pot that's too small can lead to wilting as well.

Intervention: Check the soil moisture. If dry, bottom water the plant thoroughly and allow it to soak in water via top watering. Then let it sit and drain for 30 minutes. If wet, reduce watering frequency and ensure proper drainage is provided.

Repotting into a slightly larger pot with fresh soil may be necessary in some cases. You will know that it is time for a repot by observing the roots. If the roots are growing through the drainage holes, or if you observe the roots piling up on top of each other at the bottom of the pot, it is probably time to up the size of the plant's pot and provide new soil.

Brown Leaf Tips or Edges

Cause: Brown or crispy leaf tips or edges can result from low humidity, tap water's high fluoride or chlorine content, over-fertilization or nutritional deficiencies.

Intervention: Increase humidity by using a humidifier, gathering your plants very closely together or placing the plant on a tray of wet pebbles (LECA also works well for this).

If you suspect that your tap water contains a high amount of chlorine, fluoride or salts, you can use a filter before you water your plants or let the water sit out for 24 hours to allow the chlorine to evaporate and pH levels to balance. Better yet, you can also use rainwater or distilled water.

Also be sure you aren't over-(or under-) fertilizing your plants—always follow the directions on your fertilizer of choice, ensuring you aren't using too much. Keep your plant's growing season in mind; if your plant is dormant, slow your fertilization. If you haven't been fertilizing at all or haven't repotted your plant in a long time, a potassium deficiency may be causing the discoloration. In that case, apply a balanced and high-quality fertilizer. If you suspect that the soil is depleted, consider repotting the plant in a fresh, nutrient-rich potting mix. For more on nutritional deficiencies, see page 36.

Pests

Cause: Pests like spider mites, fungus gnats, mealybugs, aphids, scale insects, thrips and whiteflies can infest houseplants. These are typically brought in unintentionally with a new plant purchase. Pests on houseplants are not always a sign of bad plant care. They happen to the best of us!

Spider mites are tiny arachnids that thrive in dry conditions. While you may not see the mites themselves, they leave telltale signs on your plant like fine webs and speckled, discolored leaves.

Fungus gnats are tiny, dark-colored flies that thrive in the moist soil conditions of houseplants. They are often seen flying around the plant or resting on the soil surface.

Mealybugs are small, white, cottony pests that infest houseplants, clustering in leaf joints and stem crevices. They feed on plant sap, leading to yellowing leaves, stunted growth and a sticky residue called honeydew, which can promote sooty mold growth.

Scale insects are small, dome-shaped pests that attach themselves to stems and leaves, feeding on sap. They often appear as brown or tan bumps.

Aphids are small, soft-bodied insects often found on houseplants, appearing in shades of green, black, brown or white. They typically cluster on the new growth and undersides of leaves, feeding on plant sap. Aphids can also excrete a sticky substance known as honeydew, which can attract other pests or lead to sooty mold growth.

Thrips are tiny, slender insects that infest houseplants, often identified by their fast movement and elongated bodies. They feed on plant sap, causing discolored flecks, streaks on leaves and distorted growth.

Intervention: First off, always quarantine new plants for two weeks before putting them near your existing collection to prevent infestation. If you know you've got a pest problem, it is always best to quarantine the affected plant away from your others. After that, treatment depends on which pest you've got:

For spider mites, the first rule of thumb is a spray down. Hose the entire plant down with pressurized water. Shower heads or sink sprayers work well for this. Next, spray the foliage and stems with an insecticidal soap or neem oil. Wipe each leaf down thoroughly with a cloth—microfiber works best. Repeat the first two steps multiple times per week for at least two weeks. Ensure good air circulation and appropriate humidity levels to deter spider mites from settling in in the future.

For fungus gnats, use sticky traps to catch the adults. You can find these at your local nursery or in many online plant shops. Additionally, mix one part of 3% hydrogen peroxide with four parts water. Water the affected plants with this solution. It will kill the gnat larvae on contact without harming your plants.

Whiteflies are winged insects often found on the undersides of houseplant leaves, feeding on plant sap. When disturbed, they create a small cloud of flying insects. Whiteflies also excrete honeydew, leading to sooty mold growth on leaves.

When treating mealybugs and scale insects, manually remove visible pests using a cotton swab dipped in rubbing alcohol. Then, apply insecticidal soap or neem oil spray to suffocate any remaining insects. Repeat applications may be necessary, as scales and mealybugs can be persistent.

To treat aphids, wipe the leaves with an insecticidal soap or neem oil. For severe infestations, consider using a systemic granule insecticide in the top layer of soil. The plant's roots will soak up the insecticide and rid the plant of pests within a few days. Regular monitoring and repeated treatments may be necessary to completely eradicate the aphids.

For thrips, rinse the leaves with pressurized water to dislodge the pests, and then apply insecticidal soap or neem oil, focusing on the undersides of leaves where thrips often reside. Wipe down each stem and leaf thoroughly. For severe infestations, consider using a systemic granule insecticide in the top layer of soil. The plant's roots will soak up the insecticide and rid the plant of pests within a few days. Regular monitoring and repeated treatments are essential to fully eradicate thrips.

To treat whiteflies, first remove heavily infested leaves. Use pressurized water to gently remove adult flies, then apply insecticidal soap or neem oil to the leaves, especially the undersides, where whiteflies congregate. Wipe each leaf and stem down individually. Repeat treatments may be necessary, and consistent monitoring is crucial to prevent reinfestation.

Prevention is key! To prevent houseplant pest infestations, start with routine inspections of your plants, especially new additions, for early signs of pests. Ensure your plants are healthy, as strong plants are less susceptible to infestations. Maintain proper watering and feeding practices to avoid stress that can attract pests. Keep humidity levels appropriate for your plants and consider using a mild insecticidal soap or neem oil spray as a preventive measure. Regularly cleaning the leaves and avoiding overcrowding of plants can also reduce the likelihood of pest problems. Remember, good plant hygiene and a watchful eye are key to keeping your indoor jungle pest-free.

Root Rot

Cause: Root rot in houseplants is primarily caused by over-watering, leading to persistently waterlogged soil. This condition creates an anaerobic (oxygen-poor) environment detrimental to roots. The lack of oxygen combined with excess moisture makes roots susceptible to fungal infections, which are the direct cause of the rotting.

Intervention: Root rot will create brown mushy roots and a foul smell coming from the pot. If root rot is suspected, remove the plant from its pot, trim away the affected roots and repot it in fresh soil. You can also soak the roots in a 2-to-1 ratio of water and 3% hydrogen peroxide for 30 minutes before repotting into fresh soil to kill the bacteria causing the rot to occur. Preventative measures include using a pot with proper drainage, choosing a well-draining soil mix and being cautious not to over-water.

Curling Leaves

Cause: Curling leaves on a plant can be indicative of a few different issues: under-watering, over-watering, temperature stress or even pests.

Intervention: If the soil is too dry, the plant will conserve water, leading to curling leaves. Check the moisture level of the soil and adjust your watering schedule accordingly to ensure you are not under-watering. Root rot can develop if the plant is over-watered and sits in water for prolonged periods. This can cause leaves to curl and yellow. Ensure the plant has proper drainage and allow the soil to dry out slightly between waterings.

If your plant is exposed to cold drafts or sudden temperature fluctuations, the leaves might curl as a response. Try to keep your plant in a stable climate to prevent shock.

And lastly, foliage-loving pests such as spider mites and mealybugs will cause the leaves to curl. Pests will keep the leaves curled for an indefinite period if not treated properly. Be sure you are regularly inspecting your plant, especially the undersides of the leaves, for creepy-crawlies!

Thinning Foliage or Leaf Drop

Cause: Thinning foliage is often due to inadequate light, pest infestation, over- or under-watering or nutrient deficiencies.

Intervention: Plants require sufficient light for photosynthesis and energy production. Lack of adequate light can lead to the shedding of leaves as the plant tries to conserve energy. Move the plant to a location where it can receive appropriate light levels. Most houseplants thrive in bright, indirect light.

Pests such as spider mites, aphids or mealybugs can weaken a plant by feeding on its sap, leading to leaf loss. Inspect the plant for signs of pests and treat accordingly with insecticidal soaps, neem oil or other appropriate methods listed in the "Pests" section (page 32).

Additionally, over-watering leads to root issues, while under-watering causes dehydration. Both issues result in foliage loss. Ensure the soil is neither too dry nor waterlogged.

Lack of essential nutrients, like nitrogen, can lead to poor foliage development and leaf drop. Use a balanced, all-purpose fertilizer to provide essential nutrients, especially during your plant's active growing season.

Slow or Stunted Growth

Cause: Slow or stunted growth could be caused by low light, nutrient deficiencies or root-bound plants.

Intervention: Make sure your plant is receiving an optimal amount of light specific to its needs. If natural lighting isn't available, consider using artificial grow lights.

Feed your plant with a balanced fertilizer as long as it is actively growing. If your plant stops growing, you can slow down your fertilizer usage.

If roots are circling the base, it's time to repot your plant. I always upsize my pot by 2 to 3 inches (5 to 7.5 cm) when repotting, but never more than that. If the pot is too large, it may retain too much water.

Leggy Growth or Stretched Stems

Cause: When plants don't receive enough light, they stretch toward the nearest light source and develop elongated stems and smaller than usual leaves. This phenomenon, known as etiolation, is the plant's natural response to low-light conditions.

Intervention: To address leggy growth, start by moving the plant to a location where it can receive more sunlight, or supplement with artificial grow lights to ensure adequate exposure.

Pruning the elongated stems can also help, as it encourages the plant to produce bushier and more compact growth.

Regularly rotating the plant ensures even exposure to light, promoting balanced growth. Additionally, continuing to care for the plant with appropriate watering and balanced nutrition will support any new growth.

Nutritional Deficiencies

Cause: Nutrient deficiencies in houseplants are often due to lack of fertilization, depleted soil or over-watering.

Intervention: Look for telltale signs like yellowing leaves (nitrogen deficiency) or brown leaf edges (potassium deficiency).

With nitrogen deficiencies, yellowing often starts with the older, lower leaves and progresses upward to the newer foliage. This is because nitrogen is a mobile nutrient, and the plant will move nitrogen from the older leaves to the newer, more active leaves when it is in short supply. When nitrogen deficient, entire leaves generally turn a uniform pale green to yellow, unlike some other nutrient deficiencies that might cause spots or patterns.

A potassium deficiency often causes browning around the edges of leaves. Potassium is crucial for maintaining turgor pressure (the water pressure inside plant cells that keeps them rigid). A deficiency compromises this, causing cells to lose their rigidity and the leaves to wilt and eventually turn brown, especially at the edges where the tissue becomes too dry.

Apply a balanced, high-quality fertilizer that provides a comprehensive range of essential nutrients, including micronutrients. If the soil is significantly depleted, consider repotting the plant in fresh, nutrient-rich potting mix to provide a healthier environment for root growth. Properly regulating your watering routine is also crucial to prevent leaching of nutrients and to maintain healthy root systems for effective nutrient uptake.

After implementing these interventions, monitor your plant closely for signs of recovery, such as improved leaf color and new growth, to ensure the measures taken are effective in addressing the deficiency.

Pale Foliage or Fading Colors

Cause: Pale or fading foliage often results from insufficient light, nutrient deficiencies (especially nitrogen), over- or under-watering or pest infestations.

Intervention: Relocate the plant to an area with more appropriate light for that specific variety. If natural light is limited, supplement with artificial grow lights to provide the necessary light spectrum.

Fertilize the plant with a balanced, all-purpose fertilizer that includes key nutrients like nitrogen, phosphorus and potassium. This will help replenish any nutrient deficiencies that might be causing the foliage to lose its vibrancy. Be mindful of the recommended dosage to avoid over-fertilization.

Adjust your watering routine to ensure the plant is neither over-watered nor under-watered. The topsoil should be allowed to dry out slightly between waterings, and the pot should have good drainage to prevent waterlogging.

Carefully inspect the plant for signs of pests. If any are found, treat the plant with an insecticide, such as insecticidal soap or neem oil. Regularly cleaning the leaves and maintaining good air circulation can also help prevent future pest infestations.

Sunburn

Cause: Sunburn in houseplants occurs when they are exposed to too much direct sunlight. This is especially common in plants that are adapted to lower light conditions and are suddenly moved to a very bright spot. The excessive light intensity can scorch the leaves, leading to discoloration, brown patches or a bleached appearance.

Intervention: If you suspect your plant is sunburned, move the affected plant to a location with indirect or filtered light. It's essential to provide a bright environment that is not too intense, especially for plants not accustomed to direct sunlight.

If you intend to expose a plant to brighter conditions, do so gradually. Incrementally increase the amount of light it receives over several weeks to allow the plant to adapt without getting burned.

Carefully remove the sunburned leaves or trim the damaged parts. This not only improves the plant's appearance but also allows it to direct energy toward new, healthy growth.

Mold or Fungus on Soil Surface

Cause: Over-watering or poor ventilation can create conditions conducive to mold or fungus growth.

Intervention: Remove the moldy top layer of soil. Allow the soil to dry out before watering again, and consider repotting if necessary. If your soil is retaining too much water, it would be wise to add some amendments such as perlite, orchid bark or LECA to improve aeration and drainage.

Be sure that the plant is receiving proper airflow, as stagnant air and humidity will always be a cause of mold.

Bottom watering might also be considered to avoid soil surface problems such as mold or fungus growth.

Lack of Blooms

Cause: Lack of blooms are often caused by insufficient light, improper fertilization, incorrect watering habits, the plant's age or dormancy period and environmental stress factors.

Intervention: To encourage your plants to bloom, start by ensuring they receive adequate natural light or supplement with grow lights for indoor plants.

Adjust your fertilization approach by using a bloom-specific fertilizer that's higher in phosphorus. Follow the recommended application schedule to promote flowering.

Regular and appropriate watering is crucial; the soil should be allowed to dry slightly between waterings, but the plant should not be left too dry or over-watered. Both extremes can affect blooming.

Understand the specific needs of your plant, including its natural flowering cycle and any age or dormancy requirements, as some plants won't bloom until they reach maturity or during certain seasons.

Additionally, creating an environment that mirrors the plant's natural habitat in terms of temperature and humidity can be beneficial. An environmentally stressed plant won't bloom.

Caring for houseplants isn't just about providing water and light; it's about observing, understanding and responding to their needs. By recognizing these common challenges and intervening appropriately, you can ensure your indoor jungle remains healthy, vibrant and thriving. Remember, each plant has its unique requirements. The more attuned you are to its signals, the better equipped you'll be to address any challenges that arise.

The Anxious Plant Parent's Guide

Many of us turn to houseplants not just as a means of beautifying our spaces but also as a soothing balm for our mental health. The presence of greenery can significantly lower stress levels, improve mood and enhance concentration. However, in our zeal to ensure the very best for our plants, we sometimes love them a little too much. Over-watering and fussing over every leaf and stem can unfortunately lead to the very outcome we strive to avoid: the demise of our beloved houseplants.

This guide aims to strike a balance, teaching you how to care gently and effectively for your plants without succumbing to the anxiety that can come with the desire to perfect their environment. Understanding the basics of plant care is crucial, but so is recognizing when our nurturing turns into smothering. By learning the signs of plant stress, adjusting our care techniques and embracing the natural ebbs and flows of plant life, we can develop a more fulfilling and less anxious relationship with our green friends.

Over-Loving Your Plants?

I Have Your Solutions!

Caring for houseplants can be an immensely rewarding experience. Their presence can transform spaces, purify the air and even uplift our moods. However, even for the completely well-intentioned plant parent, the line between care and over-care can sometimes be a blur. It's easy to smother our houseplants with too much affection, especially when we find that caring for them eases our mental ailments. Let's discuss the pitfalls of over-loving and explore alternative ways to channel that nurturing energy.

The Over-Watering Dilemma

Many plant enthusiasts, in their eagerness to ensure their plants' well-being, water them too frequently. It is always best to under-water your plant rather than over-water! Over-watering can lead to waterlogged soil, root rot and a stressed plant. Over-watering is the number one way to over-love your plants to an early grave.

Instead of reaching for the watering can whenever you feel the urge to care for your plant, adopt the "finger-test" method. Push your finger 1 inch (2.5 cm) into the soil. Only water your plant if it feels dry at that depth. If your finger-test determines that you don't need to water, you can always wipe down the leaves to help with photosynthesis or take a cutting to propagate into another plant (page 160). This should hold you over until your plant is actually craving some hydration!

Wipe Those Leaves!

If you're itching to show some love, consider giving your plants a gentle leaf cleaning. Dust on the leaves can hinder photosynthesis and block pores, making it harder for the plant to breathe.

Use a soft, damp cloth (microfiber works well) to wipe the leaves, removing dust and enhancing their shine. This not only benefits the plant but also gives you an opportunity to inspect for pests or other issues. You can take this care tactic up a notch and wipe the leaves down with a DIY leaf-shining mixture. My go-to mix is 1 cup (240 ml) of water, 1 tablespoon (15 ml) of neem oil and 10 drops of an all-natural essential oil such as eucalyptus or peppermint. This will not only shine your leaves but will also act as a pest-preventative solution.

Prune and Groom

Overgrowth can lead to leggy plants or excess dead foliage. Instead of fussing with the soil or water, focus on pruning (page 154) and propagating (page 160).

Regularly trim dead or yellowing leaves and spent flowers. This not only maintains the plant's aesthetics but also directs energy to healthier growth. You can also trim healthy stems and propagate them into a new plant! Popular methods of propagation include water propping, placing the cutting in sphagnum moss or simply potting it into a soil mix and watering thoroughly. See Propagation Made Easy (page 160) for more on this topic.

Rotate Regularly

For those who can't resist the urge to constantly interact with their plants, rotation is a great activity. Plants tend to grow toward their light source, which can result in uneven growth.

Rotate your plants every few weeks to ensure balanced growth and to give all sides equal exposure to light. If you notice a plant leaning to one side or the other, give it a 180° rotation so that it can balance itself back out with the help of light.

Dive into Plant Knowledge

Channel your enthusiasm into learning! The world of botany and horticulture is vast and fascinating.

Spend time reading about your specific plants, their natural habitats and their unique needs. The more you know, the better you can care for them without inadvertently causing harm. There are a ton of educational plant videos all across the internet. Just keep in mind, when watching these videos, not all of them are factual. Be sure to research on your own and fact check anything you see. Also remember that no two plant parents are the same—what works for you might not work for someone else and vice versa.

Create a Plant Journal

Documenting your plant's growth can be a fulfilling way to engage without overdoing direct care. Start a journal, noting watering dates, current lighting, growth spurts and any changes you observe. It's a wonderful way to track your plant's health and progress over time. This can also help you keep track of how you've been successfully (or unsuccessfully) caring for a plant so you can make any corrections necessary. You can even add little illustrations to this journal to make it more personalized and fun.

If one of your plants perishes, no worries! It's a natural part of the houseplant journey and an opportunity for learning. If a plant dies, first reflect on potential causes such as watering issues or inadequate lighting, but avoid blaming yourself. Indoor gardening involves trial and error, and even seasoned plant collectors experience losses, myself included. Consider reusing the pot and soil for a new plant, symbolizing renewal. It's also helpful to share your experience with a plant community for support and advice. Remember, caring for plants should be enjoyable, so be kind to yourself and recognize your efforts. When you feel ready, choose a new plant that suits your current skill level and apply the insights you've gained. Each new plant represents a fresh start and a chance to grow in your gardening journey!

Being an attentive plant parent is commendable, but it's essential to remember that plants, like all living things, need balance. They require periods of rest, and sometimes the best way to show love is to let them be. By channeling your nurturing tendencies into the alternatives listed above, you can ensure that your affection aids, rather than hinders, your houseplant's growth and well-being.

Traveling and Houseplants

How to Prepare Plants for Time Away

Traveling is a soul-refreshing experience that I find necessary for a well-balanced and fulfilled life, but leaving behind our plants can evoke a sense of anxiety. Plants, after all, thrive on routine care. Yet, with a bit of preparation, your indoor garden can not only survive but flourish in your absence.

I tend to over-care for my houseplants at times, especially when I am feeling anxious, and they do not appreciate my well-intentioned gestures. When I travel, I am usually gone for 7- to 10-day periods, and I find upon my return that my plants are doing much better than when I left them! I take the following steps to ensure my plants are living their best life at home while I am doing the same on my adventures away.

1. Assess the Duration and Timing

Determine how long you'll be away. A weekend trip typically requires very minimal preparation, while a journey of 7 days or more will need a bit more effort. If I am only gone for a weekend, I typically just do a once over of all of my plants to make sure the soil isn't completely dried out. If I am planning to be gone 7 days or more, I spend more time with each plant to ensure its need will be met while I am gone.

2. Water Well Before Departure

For short trips (up to a week), watering your plants thoroughly before leaving should suffice for most species. Be sure not to over-water them though! I have seen more plants perish from over-watering before a trip than I have from dry soil. Remember, it is always best to under-water rather than over-water. Ensure pots have adequate drainage to avoid waterlogged soil. Thoroughly water your plants and let the excess water drain from the bottom.

3. Group Plants Together

While humidifiers on the lowest setting will suffice for a weekend trip, they will likely run out of water for longer getaways. Clustering your plants together can help keep the humidity levels up and also prevent the soil from drying out quickly. Clustering creates a microenvironment with higher humidity, which can help keep the plants hydrated while you are away. The closeness also means they can provide some shade and protection to each other.

4. Use Self-Watering Systems

For longer getaways, self-watering systems can be lifesavers. I prefer to use one of the following options:

Water Globes or Spikes: These devices slowly release water into the soil, maintaining consistent moisture levels. However, you need to be careful when picking your device. Some globes or spikes will release water very quickly, causing the soil to become waterlogged. It is always best to buy your devices a few weeks before your trip so that you can test out the effectiveness. I prefer globes over spikes. I always read reviews or get recommendations from seasoned plant parents before deciding on which to use.

Capillary Matting: Capillary matting is a fabric that draws water from a reservoir and supplies it to the plants through capillary action. This fabric allows the plants to take up moisture through their pots' drainage holes when required. You can cut the fabric to your desired size. It is easiest to keep your mat large so that you can fit a lot of plants on it at once. I have used this method before by cutting a large rectangle (about the size of my bathtub), placing it in the bathtub and leaving a piece of the fabric in a bucket full of water to allow the mat to draw water when needed. This is a wonderful, effective way to ensure your plants will receive water for longer trips away.

5. Mulch the Soil Surface

A layer of mulch (like moss or bark) can help retain moisture in the soil, reducing the frequency of required watering. Adding 1 inch (2.5 cm) of moss or bark to the top of the soil is an acceptable way of keeping the root system moist. When you return from your trip, remove the mulch so that it doesn't keep the soil wet long-term.

6. Dial Down the Light

While plants need light, reducing their exposure can decrease their growth rate and, consequently, their water and nutrient consumption. If you're going away for an extended period, consider moving plants away from bright windows or using sheer curtains to filter the sunlight. If using adjustable grow lights, turn down the brightness to the lowest setting. This will ensure your plants aren't going to dry out as quickly as they normally would.

7. Hold Off on Fertilizing

Before going on a trip, pause fertilizing to minimize plant growth and care needs. This reduces the risk of over-feeding and stress, as plants with slower growth require less water and attention. Ideally, allow a buffer period after the last fertilization before you leave. Continuing your regular fertilization schedule upon return ensures that your plants remain stable and healthy in your absence.

8. Seek Help from a Friend

If you're away for an extended period, such as 2 weeks or more, consider having a friend or neighbor check on your plants. Provide them with a care guide (or fold over the relevant pages of this book), so they know when and how much to water. The care guide is important because a lot of our temporary caretakers might assume that your plants need water when they are actually fine! If you write your own care guide, include tips and techniques such as how to carry out the finger test for soil. This will help them understand which plants need water.

9. Automated Systems

If you're leaving for 3 weeks or more, consider investing in automated plant care systems. Timed water drip systems, humidifiers with hygrostats or smart plugs with programmable timers for grow lights can regulate the environment while you're away. I have all of my grow lights connected to smart plugs even when I am not away because it makes my life so much easier.

Post-Trip Care: Once you're back, inspect your plants for any signs of stress, pest infestation or disease. You'll be happy to see all of the new growth when you return—almost like you came home to entirely new plants. Resume your regular care routine and give them some extra love and attention by wiping down their foliage and moving them back to their normal spots in your home.

Traveling doesn't mean neglecting your indoor jungle. With thoughtful preparation, you can ensure their well-being while you explore the world. As you nurture your wanderlust, remember that your plants will be awaiting your return, ready to greet you with their new foliage.

The Plant Directory

Your Guide to Twenty Common Houseplants

Welcome to the Plant Directory—a comprehensive guide to tending to the cherished botanical residents living in our homes. Within the pages of this directory, we will be venturing into the unique universe of twenty common houseplant genera.

Though these plants may be considered "common," that does not mean they don't have specific (and sometimes tedious) care routines. We will dive into an overview of each genus, as well as different care guides and troubleshooting techniques before covering a few different varieties to search for in your local nursery, or if you're like me, a late-night online shopping sesh!

From the resilient pothos (page 51) to the delicate peperomia (page 75), the dramatic maranta (page 97) to the classic monstera (page 61), this directory will guide you through the basics of loving and understanding your houseplants' needs so that they can love you back. Each section will unveil the secrets of our green companions, providing insights into their origins, care requirements and the subtle yet impactful joys they bring into our lives.

So, as you leaf through these pages and explore the diverse characters that inhabit our homes, remember that the world of houseplants is a partnership. As we provide the care and attention these plants require, they, in turn, bestow us with their beauty, resilience and a breath of nature in our everyday lives. Whether you're a seasoned plant enthusiast or a newcomer eager to cultivate your indoor jungle, this directory is designed to serve as a trusted companion on your journey. Let's nurture our indoor oasis, one plant at a time!

Pothos

Nature's Cascading Curtain

Native to the Solomon Islands, pothos plants are known for their luscious vines, which can stretch up to 40 feet (12 m) given the right conditions. Their leaves, often variegated in hues of green, white or even yellow, bring the striking essence of the natural world to any indoor setting. Though they thrive in tropical environments, they've become synonymous with low-maintenance indoor plant care, making them ideal for those with busy lives or those just starting their plant collection.

Pothos, commonly known as devil's ivy, is the perfect gateway plant for beginner houseplant enthusiasts. These vining plants are notably resilient due to their ability to adapt to almost any lighting condition; their drought tolerance due to water storage in their foliage; and their incredible root system, which can thrive in almost any growing medium—even in water alone! They are extremely forgiving and provide lush, trailing foliage that seemingly never ends. Though these plants have been popping up everywhere from big box stores to local garden nurseries lately, pothos' winding vines and heart-shaped leaves have charmed plant enthusiasts for decades.

Note: *Some people confuse pothos plants with philodendrons (page 55). While they can have relatively similar characteristics, pothos plants differ from philodendrons primarily in their leaf shape and growth habits. Pothos leaves are generally larger and heart-shaped with distinctive variegated patterns. Philodendrons often have thinner, sometimes more deeply lobed leaves and grow both vertically and as trailing or climbing vines.*

Care Guide

Light: Survives Anywhere, Thrives in Bright, Indirect

Pothos can flourish in everything from dappled morning sun to the soft, ambient light of a north-facing room, though they will exhibit more vibrant variegation and larger foliage in the brighter areas of your home. Bright, indirect light is what your pothos is really asking you for! They can survive in dimly lit areas but might be slow to grow or lack their original variegated markings.

Hello, I am a

Pothos

 Light: Bright to Medium, Indirect

 Water: Every 1–2 Weeks

 Soil: Well-Draining, Chunky Mix

 Toxicity: Not Pet-Friendly

If placed in a dimly lit area, you will want to water your pothos less than if placed in a brighter area of your home. This is because your plant won't be photosynthesizing as quickly, therefore it will require less water to continue to produce new foliage.

Water: A Not-So-Thirsty Girl

While the pothos is more forgiving than most when it comes to occasional neglect, they do love a consistent watering routine. A consistent watering routine isn't so much about watering on a schedule as it is about observing the soil and foliage to determine if the plant needs a drink! For instance, droopy or wilting leaves are often a sign that your pothos is asking to be watered. Generally speaking, you can expect to water every 1 to 2 weeks, adjusting based on environmental factors.

When watering your pothos plants, use the "soak and dry" method. Water the plant thoroughly, allowing excess moisture to drain out of the pot, and then wait until the top 2 inches (5 cm) of soil feels dry to the touch before watering again. It's better to err on the side of too little than too much; over-watering could eventually lead to root rot.

Soil: Keep It Chunky, Keep It Happy

A well-draining mix, emulating its native tropical forest conditions, is key to keeping your pothos happy. An ideal "chunky" mix for these plants consists of 50% potting soil, 25% perlite and 25% orchid bark. These amendments to the soil will provide aeration to the roots and help prevent the plant from contracting root rot. You may also want to add compost or worm castings for a natural fertilizer.

Temperature and Humidity: Who Doesn't Like a Sauna?

Your home's conditions are likely already suitable for pothos as they enjoy temperatures between 65 to 85°F (18 to 29°C). Higher humidity is ideal for this plant, but given its resilient nature, it can thrive in your home's current humidity level. Though it would not complain if you placed a humidifier or pebble tray nearby!

Fertilization: Nom, Nom Nitrogen

A balanced, water-soluble houseplant fertilizer is suitable for pothos. The NPK ratio of 20-20-20 is often recommended. While you can use a slow-release fertilizer that is added to the soil, I wouldn't recommend it for pothos, as they don't need a lot of food for growth. If using a liquid fertilizer, be sure to add the recommended amount to the water each time you decide to fertilize.

Pothos plants don't need frequent fertilization like some of their other tropical relatives. They can be fertilized once every 1 to 2 months during the growing season (spring and summer). In the fall and winter, you can reduce fertilization to once every 2 to 3 months.

Common Problems and Solutions

1. **Yellowing Leaves:** Yellowing leaves typically point to inconsistent watering or aged foliage. Be sure you aren't over-watering or leaving a long gap in between waterings. There is a sweet spot, usually between 1 to 2 weeks! Aged, yellowing leaves will typically show up at the bottom of your pothos, closest to the soil. This is part of the plant life cycle and is completely normal. I trim these leaves off to redirect energy toward the healthier foliage and new emerging growth.

2. Leggy Vines: Most of the time, when it comes to leggy vines, it's all about the light! If your pothos gets leggy or sparse, it might not be receiving enough light. Provide your pothos with adequate lighting while also pruning the vines to stimulate new growth points at the base of the plant.

3. Curling Leaves: Curling leaves on a pothos plant are usually due to under-watering. If the soil is too dry, the plant will conserve water, leading to curling leaves. Check the moisture level of the soil and adjust your watering schedule accordingly to ensure you are not under-watering.

A Few Varieties of Pothos

Golden Pothos

The golden pothos is probably the first variety that pops into your head when you hear the word *pothos*. It is very common among big box stores and garden nurseries alike. The golden pothos is known for its green and yellow variegation and makes for an incredible starter plant because of its adaptability to almost any growing condition.

Marble Queen

Characterized by its creamy white and green marbled leaves, the marble queen is by far my favorite variety of pothos. It requires bright, indirect light to maintain its variegation, so this should be kept in mind when purchasing.

Neon Pothos

The neon pothos showcases vibrant, neon green leaves that can brighten up any room. The foliage is almost fluorescent and will maintain its vibrancy in nearly every lighting condition. If you're looking to add a pop of color to a bare space, the neon pothos is the plant for you!

Satin Pothos

Though *Scindapsus pictus*, the satin pothos, is technically not a true pothos, it's often grouped with them because of its similar appearance. It has velvety leaves with silver variegation that gives it an irresistible texture! There isn't much guessing with this plant as the foliage on the satin pothos will immediately curl when it is asking for water.

Jade Pothos

The jade pothos features solid green leaves without the variegation seen in other varieties. It is arguably the most resilient of all the varieties. I have had one living in my very dimly lit bathroom for years and it continues to give me new growth about once every two weeks.

Philodendron

Voyager of Vertical Realms

Native to the tropical Americas, philodendron plants have become a symbol of indoor botanical beauty with their unique foliage forms. Their leaves, varying from rich greens to vibrant reds, breathe life and tropical vibes into any space. Historically rooted in rainforests, they've evolved as highly sought-after indoor plants, known for their adaptability and relatively easy care. Philodendrons rank #2 on my list of all-time favorite plant genera.

Often referred to as the lover's plant due to their heart-shaped leaves and the name's Greek origin meaning "tree lover," the philodendron is an iconic choice for both novice and veteran plant enthusiasts. Their durability stems from their ability to adjust to a range of light conditions, from dappled to indirect light. Their waxy leaves aid in water retention, providing drought resistance. These plants can also thrive in various soil compositions, revealing their forgiving nature and diverse habitat adaptability. While you might spot philodendrons in numerous spaces today, from urban cafes to stylish living rooms, their timeless beauty and versatility has been loved and admired by plant enthusiasts for ages. Philodendrons remain a staple in the world of houseplants, bridging the gap between simplicity and sophistication.

Care Guide

Light: Adaptable But Happiest in Bright, Indirect

Philodendrons appreciate a broad spectrum of light conditions, from the filtered warmth of an east-facing window to the consistent glow of a room with southern exposure. While they can adapt to lower light settings, their growth might be stunted, and their iconic heart-shaped or split leaves might appear less frequently. Their love for bright, indirect light will help them produce larger, more vibrant foliage.

In dimmer spaces, these adaptable plants will have reduced photosynthetic activity, which means they will need watering less often than their counterparts residing in brighter spots. Essentially, the brighter the spot (without hours of harsh direct sunlight), the thirstier and more vibrant your philodendron will be.

Water: Drooping = Time for a Drink

Philodendrons are versatile in their care but prefer a mindful watering routine. Always look to the plant for signs: drooping leaves often hint at thirst. While many find a 1- to 2-week interval suitable, it's essential to adjust based on your plant's environment.

For the best results, use the "soak and dry" method. Water the plant thoroughly, allowing excess moisture to drain out of the pot, and then wait until the top 2 inches (5 cm) of soil feels dry to the touch before watering. Over-watering can be a culprit for problems like root rot, so it's always wise to lean toward under-watering; this applies to every plant. With philodendrons, it's about reading the plant's needs and responding accordingly.

Soil: Airy and Breathable

Philodendrons thrive in a well-aerated medium that mirrors their original rainforest habitat. A prime blend for philodendrons is made of 40% potting soil, 20% perlite, 20% orchid bark, 15% LECA and 5% worm castings. This combination ensures the roots have ample air circulation and guards against potential root rot by facilitating proper drainage with every watering.

Temperature & Humidity: Prefers High Humidity

Philodendrons are quite accommodating and will generally be content with the temperature and humidity levels in most homes. They prefer temperatures within the warm range of 65 to 85°F (18 to 29°C) and while they appreciate a humid environment, they can also adapt to less humid conditions typical of indoor settings. For those looking to provide a little extra comfort, increasing humidity with a humidifier or a pebble tray can be beneficial, but it's not a necessity for these hardy plants.

Fertilization: A Hungry, Hungry Plant

Philodendrons appreciate food with every other watering during growing season, making them a great candidate for slow-release fertilizer. However, a water-soluble fertilizer will work just as well. To support their leafy foliage, philodendron generally enjoy a balanced NPK ratio or one slightly higher in nitrogen. A common NPK ratio for philodendrons is 20-20-20 or 10-10-10, diluted to half strength.

Philodendrons can be sensitive to over-fertilization. It's crucial to follow the recommended dilution instructions on the fertilizer packaging to avoid root burn.

Common Problems & Solutions

1. **Yellowing Leaves:** Yellowing leaves in philodendrons are typically due to over-watering or aged foliage. Allow the soil to dry out between waterings, ensure the pot has proper drainage and adjust your watering schedule according to the season and indoor conditions. Regularly prune away yellow or dead leaves to redirect energy to new growth and maintain the plant's appearance.

2. **Brown Leaf Tips:** Brown leaf tips can be a sign of several underlying problems with low humidity being the most common. Philodendrons are tropical plants and thrive in higher humidity. Increase humidity around the plant using a humidifier, pebble tray with water or by grouping plants together.

3. **Curling Leaves:** Curling leaves on a philodendron can be indicative of a few different issues, with the most common being under-watering. Establish a consistent watering schedule, ensuring the soil is kept evenly moist but not waterlogged.

A Few Varieties of Philodendron

Philodendron Heartleaf

The most classic philodendron award goes to the heartleaf. This trailing plant closely resembles a pothos and is just as easy to maintain. These hardy and fast-growing plants are always a great option for beginners.

Philodendron Spadeleaf

The *Philodendron domesticum*, commonly referred to as the spadeleaf philodendron, is a striking houseplant known for its elongated, spade-shaped leaves that can grow impressively large. This low-maintenance plant is favored for its ability to adapt to a range of indoor conditions.

Philodendron Burle Marx

The philodendron Burle Marx is a distinctive and attractive houseplant, originating in the tropical regions of South America. It is known and appreciated for its elongated, heart-shaped leaves with a glossy, deep green finish, though some also have striking yellow variegation (as shown above).

Philodendron Florida Beauty

The Florida beauty is a hybrid philodendron that features a stunning array of leaves, each uniquely marked with variegations in shades of green, cream and sometimes a pale pink. The leaves are deeply segmented, almost skeleton-like in shape. Despite its stunning appearance, this plant maintains the philodendron family's reputation for being relatively easy to maintain.

Philodendron Painted Lady

Recently one of my favorite philodendrons, the painted lady is known for its bright yellow-green leaves with green speckles. As the leaves age, they turn a deeper green, contrasted by pink petioles.

Monstera

Tapestry of the Tropics

Monstera is a genus that commands attention in any indoor jungle with its dramatic fenestrated leaves. Originating from the jungles of Central and South America, these so-called Swiss Cheese plants are loved for their bold leaf structure and outstanding size. Climbing by nature, they are not only visually striking but also embody the powerful essence of the environment from which they originate.

Ranked highly among houseplant enthusiasts, myself included, monsteras are admired for their low-maintenance needs and fast growth under optimal conditions. They thrive in bright, indirect light that mimics the sunlight of their native habitat. They are also known for their resilience in less lit environments, where they may grow more slowly. Monsteras' root systems are robust and made up of long aerial roots, allowing them to draw nutrients efficiently, which contributes to their hardiness. The aerial roots can be an eye sore to those who prefer a more orderly look about their houseplants; however, I prefer to keep them as I enjoy the wild look they add to the room.

Care Guide

Light: Proper Lighting = Mature, Fenestrated Leaves

Monsteras prefer bright, indirect light but can adapt to medium light conditions. They should be protected from direct sunlight, which can burn their leaves if exposed for too long. If light is too low, new foliage may lack the characteristic fenestrations or "splits" while also unfurling smaller with each new leaf. Proper lighting supports healthy growth and leaf development in these plants, so give your monstera what it really craves: bright, indirect light! If you cannot achieve this with natural lighting, try supplementing with a grow light.

Hello, I am a
Monstera

 Light: Bright to Medium, Indirect

 Water: Every 1–2 Weeks

 Soil: Well-Draining, Chunky Mix

 Toxicity: Not Pet-Friendly

Water: Not Too Much, Not Too Little

Monsteras have water needs that are relatively straight-forward but require attention to detail to avoid common pitfalls such as over-watering. These plants like their soil to dry out partially between waterings, which generally means watering thoroughly once every 1 to 2 weeks during the active growing season in spring and summer.

In the fall and winter, when growth slows, the frequency should be reduced, and watering should occur only when the top 2 to 3 inches (5 to 7.5 cm) of soil feel dry to the touch.

Soil: The More Aeration, The Better

Monsteras thrive in a coco coir or peat-based potting mix that provides a balance of aeration, drainage and moisture retention. Just like philodendrons, a solid soil mix for monsteras is made of 40% potting soil, 20% perlite, 20% orchid bark, 15% LECA and 5% worm castings. Elements like perlite, orchid bark or LECA enhance drainage and protect against root rot. It's also beneficial for the soil to be slightly acidic to neutral in pH.

Temperature and Humidity: Think of the Tropics

Monsteras prefer a warm and humid environment, reflecting their tropical origins. The ideal temperature range for these plants is between 65 to 85°F (18 to 29°C), and they should be protected from drafts and drastic temperature changes.

While they can tolerate lower humidity levels found in most homes, they truly flourish in higher humidity. Providing humidity above 60% can promote lush growth and larger leaves. Using a humidifier or placing the pot on a tray of watered pebbles can help increase the surrounding humidity for the plant.

Fertilization: Balance is Key

Known for their large, fenestrated leaves, monsteras generally require fertilizer with every watering during their active growing season (spring and summer). A balanced, water-soluble fertilizer with an NPK ratio like 20-20-20 is suitable. A slow-release fertilizer can be used if you prefer.

Common Problems and Solutions

1. **Brown Leaf Tips:** Brown leaf tips on a monstera are typically indicative of environmental stress. The most common cause is low humidity. Increase the humidity by using a humidifier, pebble tray filled with water or grouping your monstera near other plants.

2. **Stunted Growth:** Stunted growth in monsteras is typically due to inadequate light or insufficient nutrients. Ensure your plant is receiving bright, indirect light. If natural light is insufficient, consider using grow lights. Regular fertilization during the growing season with a balanced fertilizer can provide the necessary nutrients.

3. **Leggy Stems or Small Leaves:** Leggy stems or small leaves in monsteras often result from insufficient lighting. To correct this, move your monstera to a location where it can receive bright, indirect light. This might mean positioning it closer to a window or in a brighter room. If adequate natural light isn't available, especially in darker months or in certain indoor settings, consider supplementing with grow lights.

A Few Varieties of Monstera

Monstera Deliciosa

Arguably the most popular aroid invading plant lover's homes, the *Monstera deliciosa* is collected for its large, glossy leaves with unique splits and holes called fenestrations. This tropical plant enjoys bright, indirect light and moderate watering, thriving in warm, humid environments. This was my very first houseplant, and I will forever recommend it to beginners.

Monstera Adansonii

The *Monstera adansonii*, often known as the Swiss cheese plant, is cherished for its distinctive fenestrated leaves. Known for its fast growth and vining habit, it's perfect for hanging baskets or climbing structures.

Monstera Borsigiana

The borsigiana, a close relative of the *Monstera deliciosa*, is admired for its large, heart-shaped leaves with natural fenestrations. It's a fast grower and can be trained on a trellis or left to trail, making it a versatile addition to indoor spaces. This plant is extremely easy to care for, making it beginner friendly.

Monstera Dubia

A unique and less common variety of monstera is the *Monstera dubia*. This plant is known for its smaller, heart-shaped leaves that exhibit a stunning mosaic of light and dark green. Unlike its more famous relatives, the "dubia" is a shingling plant, with its leaves lying flat against a support surface as it climbs.

Monstera Peru

The *Monstera karstenianum*, also known as monstera Peru, is a unique and eye-catching variety of monstera known for its textured, deep green, glossy leaves. Unlike the fenestrated leaves of its more famous relatives, the "Peru" has solid, heart-shaped leaves with a distinctive, almost puckered surface.

Alocasia

Veils of the Jungle

Hailing from the lush undergrowth of tropical rainforests in Asia, alocasia plants are celebrated for their striking, sculptural beauty. Characterized by their arrowhead or heart-shaped leaves that can reach dramatic proportions, these plants make a stunning statement in any indoor environment. The leaves of alocasias often display spectacular veining and come in a variety of colors and patterns, ranging from deep greens to silvery hues and variegated patterns.

Alocasias, also known as the elephant ear plant, offer a delightful challenge to the more experienced houseplant enthusiast. They are my all-time favorite houseplant to care for as they continuously challenge me with their specific needs and care requirements. These majestic plants crave a balance of consistent moisture, warmth and bright, indirect light to mimic their native jungle habitat. Their preference for high humidity and sensitivity to temperature changes can make them a bit more demanding than other houseplants. However, their rapid growth and the transformative impact they have on interior spaces make the effort worthwhile.

While alocasias may not be as beginner friendly as some other houseplants, they are incredibly rewarding for those looking to add a tropical flair to their plant collection. Their care requirements encourage plant lovers to deepen their understanding and engagement with the botanical world.

Care Guide

Light: The Perfect Spot Does Exist

Alocasias require bright, indirect light to thrive. They are adapted to the dappled sunlight of tropical rainforests, so direct sunlight should be avoided as it can scorch their leaves. However, too little light can lead to leggy growth and smaller leaves. A location near a window with filtered light or using sheer curtains to diffuse direct sunlight is ideal for these plants. If natural light is not available, supplement with artificial grow lights.

Hello, I am an

Alocasia

 Light: Bright, Indirect

 Water: Every 1–2 Weeks

 Soil: Well-Draining, Chunky Mix

 Toxicity: Not Pet-Friendly

Once you find a spot where your alocasia seems happy, try not to move it as they can be dramatic when moved! If you need to move your alocasia, try to find an area that replicates the one it was happiest in previously. An area that mimics lighting, air flow and temperature will reduce any shock. Regularly rotating the plant can also ensure even growth and leaf development.

Water: Not Too Much, Not Too Little

These plants prefer consistently moist soil, mirroring the humid conditions of their tropical rainforest habitat. They require regular watering, but it's crucial to avoid waterlogged soil to prevent root rot as it seems alocasias are more prone to rot than their other tropical friends.

Water the plant when the top 1 inch (2.5 cm) of soil feels dry to the touch, reducing frequency in winter when the plant's growth slows. Ensuring good drainage in the pot is absolutely key to the plant's overall health. Over-watering is a common issue, so it's important to find a balance that keeps the soil damp, but not soggy.

Soil: Let It Breathe

Alocasias thrive in well-draining, rich and loamy soil that retains moisture without becoming waterlogged. The mix all of my alocasias live in is 40% potting soil, 20% perlite, 20% orchid bark, 15% LECA and 5% worm castings. This composition ensures adequate drainage and aeration while providing the necessary nutrients and moisture retention. The soil should be slightly acidic to neutral in pH, something that coco coir is really great for, to mimic their natural rainforest floor habitat. Good soil structure is crucial for healthy root development and overall plant vigor in alocasias.

Temperature and Humidity: Happiest While Warm & Humid

Alocasias favor warm and humid conditions. They thrive in temperatures between 65 to 80°F (18 to 29°C). Exposure to temperatures below 60°F (15°C) can be detrimental to their health.

These plants also thrive in high humidity levels, ideally around 60% or higher. Maintaining such humidity can be achieved through using a humidifier, or placing the plant on a pebble tray with water. While they can survive in lower humidity, you may experience brown leaf edges and smaller foliage.

Fertilization: Once Every 3 Weeks

Like most plants, alocasias benefit from regular fertilization to support their lush, rapid growth. During their active growing season (spring and summer), they should be fertilized approximately once every 3 weeks with a balanced, water-soluble fertilizer. Choose a fertilizer with an equal balance of nitrogen, phosphorus and potassium (such as a 10-10-10 or 20-20-20 NPK ratio).

Over-fertilizing can lead to a buildup of salts in the soil, which can harm the plant, so it's important to adhere to a moderate and consistent fertilization schedule. It also should be noted that alocasias can drop their leaves during dormancy, and this is totally normal. They will bounce back once their surroundings warm up! During their dormant season, reduce fertilization to once every 2 months.

Common Problems and Solutions

1. Brown Leaf Tips: Brown leaf tips are often a sign of environmental stress, typically resulting from low humidity. To remedy this, increase the humidity level by using a humidifier, grouping other plants around the alocasias or placing a pebble tray with water beneath or near the plant.

2. Pests: Alocasias, with their lush foliage, are most susceptible to spider mites. If an infestation occurs, isolate the plant first before treating with insecticidal soap or neem oil. Continue treatment for several days until all signs of infestation are cleared.

3. Root Rot: Sensitive to over-watering, alocasias are particularly prone to root rot. If root rot is suspected, remove the plant from its pot, trim away the affected roots and repot it in fresh soil. You can also soak the roots in 3% hydrogen peroxide for 30 minutes before repotting into fresh soil to kill the bacteria causing the rot to occur. Preventative measures include using a pot with proper drainage, choosing a well-draining soil mix and being cautious not to over-water.

A Few Varieties of Alocasia

Alocasia Frydek

Also known as the alocasia green velvet, the Frydek is a striking houseplant renowned for its lush, velvety dark green leaves marked with prominent white or light green veins. It's dramatically pointed leaves make for a staple houseplant in any collection. A variegated Frydek was one of my first alocasias and it still charms me to this day!

Alocasia Dragon's Breath

The alocasia dragon's breath features large, glossy, deep green leaves with bold, contrasting veins. The leaves have a wavy edge and a slightly metallic sheen, creating a beautiful finish. Though still dramatic, this alocasia tends to do better in lower to moderate humidity compared to its other relatives.

Alocasia Silver Dragon

A highly sought-after plant, though much more common these days, the silver dragon boasts a silvery sheen with dark green veining. This compact variety thrives in a humid environment with bright, indirect light, making it a perfect choice for most indoor homes.

Alocasia Bambino

The bambino is a charming, compact variety of alocasia, known for its arrow-head-shaped leaves with contrasting veins. This smaller cultivar is perfect for indoor spaces, growing well in bright, indirect light and high humidity. Though this alocasia can be a drama queen, if you can figure her out, she will reward you!

Alocasia Polly

Also known as *alocasia amazonica*, the "polly" is probably the most popular variety, marked by deep green coloration and prominent white or silver veins. It thrives in bright, indirect light and requires high humidity and well-draining soil to flourish. You can find this alocasia in many big box stores.

Ferns

Ballet of Fronds

Sometimes referred to as the ancients of the plant world, ferns hold a mystique and elegance that every plant collector can appreciate. With their origins dating back to prehistoric times, ferns offer a lush throwback to the very beginnings of plant evolution. These timeless plants can transform any indoor space into a relaxing woodland sanctuary.

Ferns flourish in the soft, filtered light that mimics the forest undergrowth of their natural habitats. Their preference for high humidity and consistently moist soil reflects their tropical and temperate origins. Their care needs may intimidate some plant parents, but their rewarding foliage far outweighs their challenges!

As a plant enthusiast, I find the simplicity and diversity of ferns particularly alluring. The lack of flowers or seeds, reproducing instead through spores, adds an element that you won't find in many other plant genera. Their presence in a room brings not just a touch of nature's elegance but also a sense of connection to the ancient and unspoiled parts of our world.

Care Guide

Light: Indirect Is Your Frond

Ferns generally thrive in medium, indirect light, which mimics the amount of sunlight in their natural understory habitats in forests. Direct sunlight can scorch their delicate fronds, so it's best to place them near a window where the light is filtered through a curtain or in a spot that receives gentle morning light. Some ferns can adapt to lower light conditions, although they may not grow at a rapid rate. Ensuring the right lighting is key to maintaining the lush, green appearance of ferns.

Water: Consistency Is Key

Maintaining balance of moisture is vital to keeping ferns healthy and happy! They prefer consistent moisture and should be watered regularly, but it's crucial to avoid waterlogged soil.

Hello, I am a

Fern

 Light: Bright to Medium, Indirect

 Water: Once a week

 Soil: Rich, Well-Draining

 Toxicity: Pet-Friendly

The ideal watering routine allows the top 1 inch (2.5 cm) of soil to become slightly dry before the next watering. In environments with low humidity or during warmer seasons, they may require more frequent watering. In cooler conditions or higher humidity, they may need less. Observe your fern closely and frequently to ensure you are meeting its watering requirements.

Soil: Loose and Loamy

Ferns require soil that is well-draining and yet capable of retaining moisture. A 60/40 mix of potting soil based with coco coir or peat moss, which helps to retain moisture, and perlite or LECA for improved drainage, works well. The addition of compost or worm castings can also enrich the soil with nutrients. Ensuring the soil is aerated and not compacted is crucial, as it allows the roots to access both air and water efficiently. Any fern will thrive in a loamy, fluffy soil with air pockets formed from perlite or LECA.

Temperature and Humidity: High Humidity = Happy Fronds

Ferns typically prefer temperatures between 60 to 75°F (15 to 24°C) and struggle in temperatures below 50°F (10°C). Avoid lower temperatures to keep your fern thriving.

These fronds love their humidity! High humidity, ideally above 50%, is crucial for their well-being. In dry indoor environments, increasing humidity can be achieved through using a humidifier or placing the fern on a pebble tray with water. Frequent misting (up to three times a day) might also benefit your moisture-loving plant.

Fertilization: Dainty Appetite

Ferns require a balanced NPK ratio in their fertilizer to support healthy growth. A fertilizer with an NPK ratio of 10-10-10 or 20-20-20, diluted to half strength, is typically suitable for these plants.

Since ferns are not heavy feeders, this balanced approach, applied about once a month, provides them with the essential nutrients they need without the risk of over-fertilization. In the cooler months, reducing fertilization is best as their growth and nutrient uptake slow down.

Common Problems and Solutions

1. **Brown and Crispy Fronds:** Brown and crispy leaf edges usually indicate a lack of humidity or inconsistent watering. Increase the humidity around the fern by using a humidifier, grouping it near other plants or placing it on a pebble tray with water. Ensure a consistent watering schedule, keeping the soil evenly moist but not soggy.

2. **Yellowing Fronds:** Yellowing fronds or stems in ferns can be caused by a few different factors, with the most common being over-watering. Make sure you're allowing the top 1 inch (2.5 cm) of soil to slightly dry out before watering again. Also, be sure to use pots with adequate drainage holes and a well-draining potting mix.

3. **Pale or Leggy Fronds:** This is often a sign of inadequate light or over-fertilization. To address these issues, first assess the light conditions. Ferns prefer bright, indirect light. If your fern is in an area with too much shade, move it to a location where it can receive more light, but avoid direct sunlight, which can scorch the fronds. If the light level is appropriate, consider whether you might be over-fertilizing. Reduce the frequency of fertilization and ensure you're using a balanced, diluted fertilizer.

A Few Varieties of Ferns

Boston Fern

A classic you can almost always find hanging in a pot on a neighbor's front porch during summertime, the Boston fern is arguably the most resilient of the commonly collected ferns. Though it does love consistent moisture, it can survive a small drought here and there. This lush, delicate plant is a great place to start for beginner fern collectors.

Asparagus Fern

The asparagus fern (*Asparagus setaceus*), despite its name, is not a true fern but a member of the lily family. It's known for its feathery, light green foliage and delicate, needle-like leaves. Unlike actual ferns, this plant can be slightly toxic to pets if ingested.

Cotton Candy Fern

The cotton candy fern, known scientifically as *Nephrolepis exaltata*, is a cultivar of the Boston fern. It's admired for its fluffy, delicate fronds that resemble the soft texture of cotton candy.

Maidenhair Fern

Known for being a bit of a drama queen, maidenhair ferns are more challenging to care for due to their specific moisture and light requirements. They typically require higher levels of humidity compared to many other types of ferns to thrive; their ideal humidity level is 80%. Their fine, lacelike fronds and fan-shaped leaflets demand a strict diet of consistent moisture (by keeping the soil consistently moist) and bright, indirect lighting.

Rabbit's Foot Fern

The rabbit's foot fern is a unique fern variety distinguished by its furry rhizomes that resemble rabbit's feet, often seen creeping over the edge of the pot. These rhizomes help store moisture, making the plant somewhat drought-tolerant and easier to care for than a lot of its family members.

Peperomia

Petite Mosaics

Originating from the lush rainforests of South America, peperomia plants boast over a thousand species, each with unique and often strikingly patterned leaves. Their foliage, coming in a fun array of shapes, sizes and colors, ranges from deep greens to more elaborate variegations, incorporating shades of red, gray and cream.

Peperomia, commonly referred to as radiator plants, are perfect for enthusiasts starting their journey into the world of houseplants. They stand out for their adaptability to a variety of indoor conditions, still growing in medium to low light and requiring minimal watering, thanks to their succulent-like leaf structure that retains moisture. While they are adaptable and can survive in less humid conditions typical of many homes, providing some extra humidity can promote lush growth and vibrant foliage. This makes them particularly forgiving and low-maintenance, ideal for those with busy lives.

Care Guide

Light: Extremely Adaptable

Peperomia plants are quite versatile when it comes to their light requirements, thriving in a range of lighting conditions from medium to bright, indirect light. They are ideally suited for spots that receive filtered sunlight, such as near east- or west-facing windows where the light is gentle. The variegated types of peperomia particularly benefit from brighter light to maintain their vibrant colors.

While peperomias can adapt to lower light conditions, they may not thrive, potentially leading to less vibrant foliage and slower growth. In areas with lower light, it's important to adjust your watering schedule accordingly. Less light means slower photosynthesis, so the plant will use less water.

 Light: Bright to Medium, Indirect

 Water: Every 1–2 Weeks

 Soil: Rich, Well-Draining

 Toxicity: Pet-Friendly

Water: Less Is More

With their semi-succulent qualities, peperomia have a moderate tolerance for drought, making them relatively low-maintenance in terms of watering. They prefer the soil to slightly dry out between waterings. Over-watering can be detrimental, leading to issues like root rot, so it's important to ensure that the soil isn't kept constantly wet! A good rule of thumb is to water your peperomia when the top 2 inches (5 cm) of the soil feels dry to the touch.

Soil: Semi-Chunky, Mostly Loamy

Peperomias flourish best in a well-draining soil mix that mimics the slightly moist yet well-aerated conditions of their native habitat. An ideal potting mix for peperomias is one that combines regular potting soil with elements that enhance drainage and aeration, like perlite and orchid bark. A recommended blend might be 60% potting soil, 20% perlite and 20% orchid bark. This mix ensures that the roots of your peperomia receive sufficient air and water without the risk of waterlogging, a common cause of issues like root rot in these plants.

Temperature and Humidity: Ideal Terrarium Plants

These plants thrive in typical indoor temperature ranges, preferring environments that stay between 65 to 75°F (18 to 24°C). They are sensitive to extreme cold and should be protected from drafts and temperatures below 50°F (10°C).

Peperomia plants originate from tropical and subtropical regions, so they enjoy moderate to high humidity levels. However, they are quite adaptable and can tolerate the lower humidity levels commonly found in homes. If you want to keep your peperomia extra happy, keep them near a humidifier or pebble tray with water! They also make lovely terrarium plants as they remain smaller in size and thrive in the extra humidity.

Fertilization: Light and Balanced

Peperomia plants benefit from a light feeding about once a month during the growing season (spring and summer) using a diluted, balanced (10-10-10 or 20-20-20 NPK ratio), water-soluble fertilizer. Over-fertilization can harm these plants, so it's important to use a half-strength solution. If you notice the growth slowing down during the cooler months, reduce fertilization.

Common Problems and Solutions

1. **Over-Watering:** Peperomias have semi-succulent characteristics, meaning their leaves and stems can store water. To prevent over-watering, be sure you are letting the top 2 inches (5 cm) of soil dry out between waterings. If you feel the urge to water your peperomia when it's not yet ready, try something like dusting the leaves or taking a cutting instead!

2. **Low Humidity:** Signs of low humidity stress include brown, crispy leaf edges, dull or lackluster foliage and slowed growth. To increase the humidity in your indoor setting, consider adding a humidifier or pebble tray near your moisture-loving plants. A humidifier will be most effective at raising humidity levels a considerable amount. You can also group your peperomia near other plants to increase the humidity levels in the area.

3. Leggy Growth: Leggy growth in peperomia plants typically occurs when the plant is not receiving adequate light. Remedy leggy growth by providing proper lighting for your peperomia. If natural lighting isn't an option, consider supplementing with a grow light. You can also prune back the leggy stems to encourage a bushier plant. Don't throw the cuttings away; root them in water! You can add these back into the plant pot to quickly achieve a fuller look.

4. Pests: The most common pests that peperomia encounter are spider mites. Spider mites can be hard to spot, especially if your peperomia displays multiple colors. If you notice spider mites, be sure to isolate your plant. Hose it down with pressurized water. Using an insecticidal soap or neem oil is a great way to rid your plant of mites while an increase in humidity and airflow can help keep them gone.

A Few Varieties of Peperomia

String of Turtles

Possibly the most popular peperomia, the string of turtles is particularly admired for its small, round leaves that resemble turtle shells and feature intricate patterns of green, white and sometimes purple. This plant produces small, spike-like flowers that are white to pale cream in color. These flowers, often called "rat tail" flowers, are subtle compared to the plant's distinctive, turtle shell-patterned leaves. Relatively easy to maintain, it is a great starter "string of" plant for beginners.

Watermelon Peperomia

The watermelon peperomia's round, fleshy leaves resemble the rind of a watermelon. The foliage is marked with patterns of dark green and silver stripes. This small and super cute plant typically grows up to 8 inches (20 cm) tall and is perfect for tabletops or shelves.

Peperomia Metallica

My favorite peperomia I've come across so far is the metallica. The leaves are typically a deep green or reddish-purple color with a distinctive metallic shimmer and prominent veining, often with a contrasting red or pink underside. This particular variety can easily become leggy, so regular pruning is recommended to keep its bushy appearance.

Ripple Peperomia

A popular choice among houseplant enthusiasts because of its easygoing nature, the ripple peperomia is a great choice for beginners. The leaves feature a unique, ripple-like pattern, giving them a corrugated appearance, and come in various shades from green to silver and even red.

Raindrop Peperomia

Raindrop peperomia's name comes from the shape of its leaves, which resemble raindrops or teardrops—large, glossy and heart-shaped with a pointed tip. This small, compact plant is a lovely addition to any shelf or desk needing some greenery.

Nerve Plant

Nature's Nervous System

Nerve plants, scientifically known as fittonias, are enchanting plants native to the tropical rainforests of South America. They are loved for their richly veined and vibrantly colored leaves. The intricate network of white, pink or red veins against the dark green foliage resembles the human nervous system, hence the name nerve plant.

Discovered in the 19th century by botanists Elizabeth and Sarah Mary Fitton, the plant was later named fittonia in their honor. Thriving under the dense canopy of the rainforest, fittonias developed striking leaf patterns and colors as adaptations to the low-light conditions of their native environment. These adaptations make them well-suited to indoor living, where they bring a splash of tropical vibes to any setting. Because these plants are lovers of humidity, many plant enthusiasts enjoy watching nerve plants thrive in terrarium setups.

Nerve plants can be extremely dramatic when under-watered, wilting over within a matter of hours. The untrained eye may presume them perished, but they are just asking for a drink! Once watered, the plant usually pops back up just as quickly as it wilted.

Care Guide

Light: Think Dappled Forest Floor

Nerve plants thrive in medium, indirect lighting. They are natively used to the dappled lighting of the forest floor, so bright, direct lighting would be too much for their foliage to handle.

An ideal location for a nerve plant would be near a window that receives plenty of natural light but is shielded from direct sunrays, such as a spot with a sheer curtain. The soft morning sunshine or ambient light from east- or north-facing windows, respectively, typically provide a suitable light environment. If natural light is limited in your space, consider using grow lights to provide sufficient illumination.

Hello, I am a

Nerve Plant

 Light: Bright to Medium, Indirect

 Water: Once a Week

 Soil: Rich, Well-Draining

 Toxicity: Pet-Friendly

Water: Dramatic When Thirsty

These plants require consistently moist soil, but it's important to avoid over-watering to prevent root rot. Water nerve plants when the top 1 inch (2.5 cm) of soil feels slightly dry, ensuring frequent but moderate watering. If they go too long without water, they will become limp and fall over!

Be mindful of the signs of over-watering, such as yellowing leaves, and adjust accordingly. Using pots with drainage holes and a well-draining soil mix is essential. Regular soil moisture checks and adjusting your watering routine based on your home's specific conditions will help maintain the health of your fittonia.

Soil: Rich and Loamy

Nerve plants thrive in well-draining, rich and moist soil. A potting mix that retains moisture while still allowing excess water to drain away is ideal. A good blend for fittonias can include a mix of 60% potting soil, which holds moisture well, and 40% perlite or LECA, which improves drainage. This combination helps mimic the plant's natural habitat on the rainforest floor, providing the necessary balance between moisture retention and drainage. Ensuring the soil is aerated and not overly dense is key to supporting the plant's root health and overall growth.

Temperature and Humidity: The More Moisture, the Better

They have a preference of warm and humid conditions, typical of their native tropical rainforest environment. They thrive in temperatures between 65 to 80°F (18 to 29°C). Temperatures below 60°F (15°C) can be harmful to the plant, so it's important to protect them from cold drafts and sudden temperature fluctuations.

High humidity is crucial for nerve plants, ideally around 50 to 60% or higher. In drier indoor environments, humidity can be increased by misting the plant regularly (up to three times a day), using a humidifier or placing the plant on a pebble tray filled with water.

Fertilization: Not So Hungry

Nerve plants benefit from regular but light fertilization. During their active growing season (spring and summer), feeding them with a balanced (10-10-10 or 20-20-20 NPK), water-soluble fertilizer diluted to half strength once a month supports their growth.

It is important to avoid over-fertilizing, as this can lead to a buildup of salts in the soil, which can harm the plant. If growth slows during the fall and winter, reduce the frequency of fertilization.

Common Problems and Solutions

1. **Wilting Leaves:** Wilting leaves in fittonia are most commonly caused by under-watering and low humidity. Ensure the plant is watered regularly, allowing the top 1 inch (2.5 cm) of soil to dry slightly between waterings.

2. **Leggy Growth:** Nerve plants experience leggy growth when they have insufficient light. To correct this, increase exposure to bright, indirect light, such as near a window with sheer curtains. Regular pruning of leggy stems can encourage bushier growth, and rotating the plant ensures even light distribution. If natural light is inadequate or you don't have a great window in your home, consider using grow lights.

3. Pests: Nerve plants can be affected by many pests, but the most common is definitely mealybugs. I use a cotton swab dipped in isopropyl alcohol to treat these pests. Wipe them off individually and spray down the plant with an insecticidal soap for good measure. Treatment may be needed more than once to eradicate the pests entirely.

4. Crispy Leaf Edges: Crispy leaf edges usually indicate low humidity. Increase humidity around the plant with a humidifier, grouping plants close to each other or a pebble tray.

A Few Varieties of Nerve Plants

Ruby Red

The ruby red nerve plant, arguably the most common variety, is known for its vibrant reddish-pink veining against dark green leaves. This ornamental foliage, with its network of bright, saturated lines, creates a lovely visual contrast that makes the plant a popular choice for plant collectors.

Skeleton

This unique variety has thin, pronounced pink veins that almost look like a skeletal structure, hence the name. The green leaves are rich in color, making the pink veining stand out even more.

Pink Angel

The pink angel nerve plant features eye-catching pink veins against deep green leaves. Its unique pink foliage makes it a common choice for house-plant enthusiasts seeking a vibrant and easy-to-care-for plant.

Leather Leaf

A distinctive variety of fittonia, the leather leaf is known for its robust and textured foliage. The leaves have a deep green color and a leathery, rugged texture, contrasted with veins that can be white, pink or red.

Frankie

This variety stands out for its ruffled edges and green speckled leaves. The foliage differs from other nerve plant varieties because of the unique shape each leaf presents. If you love nerve plants, this is a must-have for your collection!

Ficus

Sovereign of Silk Foliage

Welcome to the diverse and elegant world of ficus, a genus that comprises some of the most beloved and adaptable plants in the indoor gardening realm. Ficus plants, with their origins spanning across multiple continents from Asia to Africa and Australia, come in an incredible array of forms, from the iconic fiddle-leaf fig to the popular tineke ficus. Each species brings its unique aesthetic to both home and office, making them a mainstay in interior plant design.

Loved for their lush foliage, ficus plants can serve as focal points or complementary greenery in various settings. While they are known for their resilience and adaptability to indoor environments, they each have specific care requirements that ensure their health and vitality. With some varieties reaching heights upward of 6 feet (1.8 m) tall, ficus plants can easily make themselves the focal point of any room! Whether you are a seasoned plant enthusiast or a beginner eager to "green" your space, ficus plants offer both the beauty and the challenges that make indoor gardening a rewarding experience.

Care Guide

Light: Happiest in Bright, Indirect

Ficus plants generally need bright, indirect light. They flourish near windows that offer sunlight without direct midday exposure, which can burn their leaves. East- or west-facing windows are typically recommended. If bright, indirect light cannot be achieved through natural lighting, supplementing with a grow light is a great idea.

Some ficus varieties, such as *Ficus maclellandii*, *Ficus elastica* and the fiddle-leaf fig can tolerate lower light but may grow more slowly and lose leaf color. Observing the plant's response to light and adjusting its position is key to a happy ficus!

Water: Observe the Soil

These plants prefer their soil to dry out slightly between waterings. You should water your ficus when the top 2 inches (5 cm) of soil feels dry to the touch. This is the best way to determine if you need to water the plant. The second-best way to know is if you observe the leaves starting to droop. If this is the case, your plant is probably several days overdue for a drink.

Over-watering can lead to root rot, so ensure good drainage. Water less in winter when the plant's growth slows down. The frequency of watering will vary based on environmental conditions like light, temperature and humidity.

Soil: Well-Draining But Water-Retaining

Ficus plants thrive in well-draining, nutrient-rich soil. A good mix for ficus should consist of a combination of 50% potting soil, 25% orchid bark and 25% perlite, which ensures adequate drainage while retaining enough moisture. This type of soil mix helps prevent issues like root rot, which can occur in overly wet conditions. It's also beneficial to choose a soil that slightly holds onto water, as ficus plants don't like to dry out completely.

Temperature and Humidity: Warmth and Mist = Ficus Bliss

They prefer temperatures between 60 to 75°F (15 to 24°C) and moderate to high humidity, though they can survive in lower humidity. Ficus should be protected from sudden temperature changes and cold drafts as this can shock them.

To increase humidity and happiness, especially in dry conditions such as wintertime, use a humidifier or place the plant on or near a pebble tray with water. You should avoid placing ficus near heating vents, air conditioners or cold windows to maintain a stable and suitable environment.

Fertilization: Appreciates a Light Feeding

Ficus plants benefit from regular fertilization, but with a light touch! During their growing season in spring and summer, a balanced (10-10-10 or 20-20-20 NPK), water-soluble fertilizer diluted to half strength should be applied about once a month. This provides the necessary nutrients without overwhelming the plant.

In the fall and winter, if the plant's growth naturally slows, reduce fertilization. Over-fertilization can lead to salt buildup in the soil, which can harm the ficus, so it's important to fertilize with this in mind.

Common Problems and Solutions

1. Leaf Drop: Leaf drop in ficus plants often results from environmental stress, such as changes in location, temperature fluctuations or inconsistent watering. Leaf drop is the most common issue that ficus face living indoors. To prevent this, be sure you are providing a stable environment with consistent light and temperature. It is also important to establish a good watering routine. This doesn't mean to water the same amount on the same day; this means to observe the soil and foliage consistently to see if it needs a drink. If moving the plant, do it gradually to allow acclimation. After addressing these factors, give the ficus time to stabilize and recover from stress. Moving plants can be one of the most stressful actions to take, so it is always best to do so slowly.

2. Yellowing Leaves: Yellowing leaves are often due to over-watering or under-watering. Ensure you are letting the soil dry slightly between waterings and ensure good drainage. Adjust your watering routine, if necessary. You can use a moisture meter, chopstick or just your finger to see how saturated the soil is down below.

3. Brown Leaf Edges: Brown leaf edges in ficus plants are often a sign of low humidity. You can use a humidifier to consistently raise the air moisture around your plant or group your plants together. Another option is to place the plant on or near a pebble tray filled with water.

4. Pests: The most common pests I have come across on my ficus plants are spider mites. If you experience spider mites on your ficus, isolate the plant and use a pressurized water spray to remove mites, followed by treatments with insecticidal soap or neem oil. Multiple applications may be needed until the infestation is cleared. You can also increase humidity and airflow around the plant to help keep these pests away.

A Few Varieties of Ficus

Ficus Tineke

A cultivar of the popular *Ficus elastica* (rubber plant), the tineke is collected for its variegated foliage. The leaves are glossy and broad, featuring a beautiful blend of green, cream and pink hues. Like other *Ficus elastica* varieties, the tineke grows upright and can become quite tall, making it an excellent choice for a floor plant in homes or offices.

Fiddle-Leaf Fig

The fiddle-leaf fig is a highly sought-after houseplant, famous for its large, glossy, violin-shaped leaves. Though this plant is sold in almost every big box store these days, it can be one of the most dramatic to own and maintain. Known for its somewhat finicky nature, the fiddle-leaf fig demands stable conditions without extreme changes in temperature or light.

Ficus Umbellata

The umbellata is a lesser known but visually stunning member of the ficus family. It stands out for its large, umbrella-like leaves, which are broad, round and richly green, creating a canopy effect.

Banana Leaf Fig

The banana leaf fig, known scientifically as *Ficus maclellandii* "alii," is an attractive and less common variety of the ficus family. It grows long, narrow leaves that resemble a banana leaf, giving it an elegant appearance. Its unique foliage and ease of care make it a great option for those looking to diversify their indoor plant collection with a less conventional ficus variety.

Ficus Burgundy

The *Ficus elastica* Burgundy is a dark variety of the rubber plant family. It produces glossy dark green leaves that can appear almost black. Its deep burgundy undertones give it a striking appearance. The ficus Burgundy's deep, moody coloring makes it my all-time favorite variety.

Calathea

Nature's Dancer

Native to the tropical Americas, calatheas are admired by plant lovers because of their intricate patterns, colors and especially their movements. From the pinstripe designs on the leaves of the *Calathea ornata*, to the contrast and surprising ease of care found in the rattlesnake calathea, each species offers a unique display of natural beauty, but we can't forget their dramatics! They are also known as some of the most difficult plants to keep happy, or even semi-happy. They require quite specific care techniques in order to truly thrive in our homes.

Calatheas have the remarkable ability to move their leaves in response to light, a phenomenon that adds an almost magical dynamic to their presence. In the evening, their leaves often fold up, resembling hands in prayer, only to spread wide again with the morning light. Oftentimes, you can see and hear the movement of these plants.

Calatheas are more than just visually appealing; they are also known for their air-purifying qualities, making them a functional addition to any indoor space. While they are celebrated for their beauty, they do require a bit more attention compared to other houseplants. If you like a challenging houseplant, I definitely recommend a calathea.

Care Guide

Light: Gentle, Dappled Lighting

Calathea plants thrive in bright, indirect light. Direct sunlight can scorch their leaves, while too dim light can cause their vibrant patterns to fade. Your calathea will be happiest in a well-lit area of your home. If you can't provide the natural lighting a calathea needs to thrive, supplement with a grow light. Ensuring the right light balance is crucial for maintaining the vividity and health of their foliage.

Hello, I am a
Calathea

 Light: Bright, Indirect

 Water: Once a Week

 Soil: Rich, Well-Draining

 Toxicity: Pet-Friendly

Water: Thirsty for Consistent, Gentle Sips

Water calatheas when the top 1 inch (2.5 cm) of soil feels slightly dry, maintaining consistent moisture without overwatering. There is a happy medium when it comes to the amount of water in their soil. If you can find that, they will reward you!

They prefer soft, lukewarm water, ideally distilled or rainwater, to avoid leaf damage from harsh chemicals in tap water. If your tap water is hard, you will almost always experience brown edges on the foliage. Leave out your tap water overnight to let the chlorine evaporate before feeding it to your calathea. Regular checks of soil moisture are crucial to their care.

Soil: Think Rich Forest Floors

Calatheas flourish in soil that strikes a perfect balance between moisture retention and drainage. A mix that blends peat moss or coco coir with elements like perlite or LECA creates an ideal environment, ensuring the soil stays aerated yet moist. A combination of 65% peat or coco-based potting mix with 35% perlite or LECA would work well. You can also add in compost or worm castings for a natural fertilizer.

This combination mimics the natural, humid conditions of their rainforest origins, providing the right foundation for healthy root development and vibrant growth. Their roots are typically thin in nature, so having something to grab onto such as the perlite or LECA really enhances their health and overall resilience.

Temperature and Humidity: Rainforest Vibes Preferred

Calatheas flourish in warm environments, preferring temperatures between 65 to 85°F (18 to 29°C), and require protection from cold drafts and sudden temperature changes. Unless particularly drafty, your home's current temperature is probably okay for a calathea.

High humidity, around 50 to 60% or higher, is also essential for their happiness and well-being. Many varieties can become very dramatic and perish quickly if their humidity needs are not met. In dry indoor settings, using a humidifier or placing it on or near a pebble tray filled with water can help maintain the necessary humidity levels for these tropical natives.

Fertilization: Mindful Balance

A balanced, water-soluble fertilizer with an NPK ratio of 10-10-10 or 20-20-20, diluted to half its strength, is recommended for calatheas. While they require a bit more nourishment compared to plants like pothos, careful application is key. For liquid fertilizers, follow the mixing instructions and apply it during your regular watering routine. Since these plants are very sensitive to being over-fertilized, slow-release granules are not recommended.

Calatheas should be fertilized monthly during the growing season (spring and summer) when they are most active. In the fall and winter, if growth slows, reduce the frequency of fertilization to once every 2 to 3 months. This fertilization schedule ensures that your calathea receives sufficient nutrients without the risk of over-feeding.

Common Problems and Solutions

1. Brown Leaf Edges: Brown leaf tips and edges in calathea might be the most common issue plant lovers deal with. This is often due to low humidity or watering with hard tap water. Elevate the humidity around your calathea to replicate its tropical habitat. This can be done by using a humidifier or placing the plant on a pebble tray with water. Grouping plants together can also naturally increase humidity. You can also mist your calathea to help with humidity, though this is the least effective method. If you're using tap water, the fluoride and chlorine content might contribute to brown leaf tips. Switching to filtered or distilled water can mitigate this problem.

2. Yellowing Leaves: Yellowing leaves in calathea plants usually indicate over-watering. You should let the top 1 inch (2.5 cm) of soil dry out before watering again. Ensure your pot has adequate drainage holes and use a well-draining soil mix to prevent water from accumulating at the roots. If water accumulates frequently, it could lead to root rot.

3. Curling Leaves: Curling leaves in calathea plants can be a symptom of under-watering or low humidity. Water your calathea when the top 1 inch (2.5 cm) of soil feels dry, ensuring the soil is evenly moistened but not saturated. Adjust how many times you are checking on your plant to ensure this doesn't happen! Being native to tropical climates, calatheas thrive in high humidity. Enhance humidity by placing a humidifier nearby, grouping plants together or setting it on a pebble tray with water. This can help prevent leaves from curling due to dry air.

4. Pests: Spider mites are by far the most common pests plant lovers deal with on their calathea. To treat, first isolate your calathea. Then, hose the entire plant down with pressurized water. Apply insecticidal soap or neem oil, focusing on the undersides of the leaves where mites congregate. Regular applications may be necessary until the infestation is fully controlled.

A Few Varieties of Calathea

Pinstripe Calathea

Scientifically known as *Calathea ornata*, this calathea is admired for its striped, almost fake-looking foliage. Its dark green leaves are marked with thin, delicate pink to white lines, resembling the pinstripes of a suit, giving it a distinct appearance.

Rattlesnake Calathea

The rattlesnake calathea is known to be one of the easier varieties to care for. The long, wavy leaves are green with a pattern of dark green spots and stripes on top and a deep purple underside, resembling the skin of a rattlesnake. The rattlesnake calathea is a popular choice for its easygoing nature.

Network Calathea

The network calathea, or *Calathea musaica*, stands out with its intricate, network-like pattern of fine lines on bright green leaves, creating a mosaic effect. This stunning foliage makes it a visually captivating houseplant. This is by far the easiest calathea to care for, in my opinion. They don't mind low humidity and can tolerate the occasional hard tap water!

Medallion Calathea

The medallion is known for its round, patterned leaves with dark green markings and purple undersides. It thrives in bright, indirect light and high humidity. This plant is popular for its distinctive leaf design and ability to enhance indoor spaces with its lush appearance.

Dottie Calathea

The dottie calathea, with its deep green to almost black leaves and striking pink markings, stands out for its bold appearance. This plant's unique color contrast and lush foliage make it a popular choice for those looking to add a vibrant, eye-catching element to their indoor plant collection.

Maranta

Harmonizer of Day and Night

Commonly known as the prayer plant, the maranta is a captivating addition to anyone's indoor jungle. Native to the tropical rainforests of Brazil, marantas are cherished for their moving foliage. Mimicking their very similar relative calathea, their leaves display a mesmerizing dance, folding up in the evening and unfolding with the morning light. Their leaves are a canvas of painted patterns, often show-casing a mix of deep greens, bright reds and creamy whites.

The Prayer Plant's intriguing leaf movements and foliage patterns make it a fasci-nating subject for indoor gardeners. While thriving in the understory of rainforests, marantas have adapted remarkably well to indoor environments, asking for bright, indirect light and consistent moisture to mimic their natural habitat. Their non-toxic nature makes them a safe and delightful choice for homes with pets.

Marantas can be picky with their care routines, so studying up on their individual desires is beneficial before bringing them into your home. They are moisture-loving plants with an appetite for filtered water. Though sometimes dramatic, they can also be extremely rewarding once the proper care routine is established!

Care Guide

Light: Thriving in Bright, Indirect Light

Maranta plants prefer an environment with bright but indirect sunlight. They can adapt to medium, indirect light, though their vivid leaf patterns might become less pronounced. Direct sunlight can be harmful, so keep them out of the harsh UV rays! If placed in lower light, you will likely need to water your maranta less.

Placing them in a spot that receives filtered morning light, such as near an east-facing window, is ideal. If this isn't possible, consider supplementing with a grow light.

Hello, I am a

Maranta

 Light: Bright, Indirect

 Water: Once a Week

 Soil: Rich, Well-Draining

 Toxicity: Pet-Friendly

Water: Regular Sips

These plants require consistent moisture, so water them when the top 1 inch (2.5 cm) of soil dries out. Be thorough yet cautious with watering, as over-watering can lead to root rot.

The need for water varies with environmental conditions, often increasing in warmer seasons. As with most plants, you will need to water more during the warmer months and less during the cooler. Use pots with drainage holes to prevent water accumulation and check the soil regularly to maintain the ideal balance between moisture and drainage for your maranta.

Soil: Rich and Well-Aerated

Marantas prefer a well-draining, rich soil that retains some moisture. A potting mix incorporating peat moss or coco coir, which helps retain moisture, along with perlite or LECA for improved drainage, works well. This composition ensures the roots have access to both air and moisture, essential for healthy growth. Like calathea, marantas would like 65% potting mix with 35% perlite or LECA. You can also add in compost or worm castings for a natural fertilizer.

Temperature and Humidity: Warm, Misty Vibes

Maranta plants prefer a warm and humid environment. They thrive at temperatures between 65 to 80°F (18 to 26°C) and should be protected from cold drafts and sudden temperature fluctuations. Keep them away from air vents in your home in order to maintain a stable environment.

High humidity is crucial for marantas, ideally around 50 to 60% or higher. They thrive in tropical rainforest-like conditions. To increase humidity, you can use a humidifier or place the plant on or a near a pebble tray with water.

Fertilization: Balanced Food, Happy Foliage

Marantas are appreciative of a meal once a month. During the growing season (spring and summer), feed them with a balanced (10-10-10 or 20-20-20 NPK), water-soluble fertilizer, diluted to half the recommended strength once a month. This provides essential nutrients without overwhelming the plant.

If growth slows in the cooler months of fall and winter, reduce fertilization. Over-fertilization can harm marantas, so it's important to fertilize judiciously. If you notice burn marks, you might be over fertilizing!

Common Problems and Solutions

1. **Brown Leaf Edges:** Crispy, brown edges in maranta plants prove to be a very common issue and typically result from low humidity or hard tap water. Use a humidifier or place the plant on a pebble tray to increase humidity. You can also group plants together to increase humidity in the area. Misting your maranta might help to increase moisture but would need to be carried out at least two times a day to make a difference. These plants can be drama queens about their water! If you're using tap water, the fluoride and chlorine content might contribute to brown leaf tips. Switching to filtered or distilled water will solve this problem. If this is not an option, leave your watering can of tap water sitting out overnight to let the chlorine evaporate.

2. **Yellowing Leaves:** Yellowing leaves in maranta plants are often due to over-watering. To address over-watering, water only when the top 1 inch (2.5 cm) of soil is slightly dry and ensure the pot has proper drainage. Consider repotting in well-draining soil, if necessary.

3. Curling Leaves: Curling leaves are common in maranta plants and usually indicate under-watering or low humidity. Water the plant when the top 1 inch (2.5 cm) of soil dries out. Adjust your watering routine to ensure the plant is receiving an adequate amount of water each week. You can increase humidity through the use of a humidifier or a pebble tray as well as group other plants around your maranta. It will thank you for the added moisture!

4. Pests: Spider mites are typically what collectors deal with when it comes to maranta pests. If you notice mites, isolate the plant first. Then, hose the entire plant down with pressurized water. Apply insecticidal soap or neem oil, focusing on areas where mites are prevalent, like the undersides of leaves. You may need to apply these treatments regularly to fully eradicate the mites. Increase humidity and airflow around the plant to deter spider mites.

Common Varieties of Maranta

Lemon Lime

The lemon lime maranta produces leaves with a unique blend of bright green and yellow hues, resembling the colors of a lemon and a lime. This maranta variety is one of the most popular, making frequent appearances in local nurseries and big box stores.

Silver Band

A distinct variant of the prayer plant family, the silver band is a widely collected houseplant. The leaves are deep green with a silver band running along the midrib, creating a beautiful contrast. The silver band maranta is an excellent choice for adding a touch of sophistication to indoor plant collections.

Cristata

With its paint-stroke dots and oval leaf shape, the *Maranta cristata* is a common plant collected. This variety requires moderate to bright, indirect light and consistent moisture to thrive, making it an ideal choice for plant enthusiasts willing to provide attentive care.

Rabbit's Foot

This maranta is known for its appealing green leaves marked with distinctive brown patches that resemble rabbit footprints. The rabbit's foot maranta is a popular choice for its unique foliage pattern.

Red

Often known as the red prayer plant, the red maranta is distinguished by its beautifully painted leaves. The foliage combines deep green with red veins and sometimes light green or yellowish patches.

Orchid

Orchidaceae Elegance

Originating from diverse environments across the globe, orchids have become an obsession for some plant lovers because of their breathtaking flowers, which can display a spectacular array of colors and forms. These exotic blooming plants, often found in tropical rainforests, mountainous regions and even grasslands, bring the allure of far-off places into our everyday lives. Orchids have gained popularity for their ability to flourish under indoor conditions, with some species fitting seamlessly into the lives of both seasoned collectors and novice plant enthusiasts.

Orchids, encompassing a vast family known as *Orchidaceae*, are often seen as the crown jewels of the plant world. Their adaptability to a range of indoor environments, along with specific but manageable watering needs, makes them a wonderful choice for plant lovers. They have a unique ability to thrive in a variety of growing mediums, from specialized orchid bark to moss, showcasing their versatility.

Whether displayed in a simple pot or as part of a more elaborate arrangement, they bring a touch of sophistication and natural beauty to any setting. Orchids offer a rewarding experience for those who delve into their care and have become a beloved mainstay in the world of houseplants.

Care Guide

Light: Bright and Filtered

Orchids generally thrive in bright, indirect light. Direct sunlight can be too harsh and burn their growing foliage, while insufficient light can hinder their ability to bloom. Since blooms are the goal when buying an orchid, it is best to give them sufficient bright, indirect lighting.

A spot near an east- or south-facing window covered with a sheer curtain is ideal, providing gentle light without the intensity of direct, midday sun. If this lighting is not achievable, supplement with a grow light. Just remember that lighting is the main factor in helping orchids bloom!

Hello, I am an
Orchid

 Light: Bright to Medium, Indirect

 Water: Every 1–2 Weeks

 Soil: Orchid Bark

 Toxicity: Pet-Friendly

Water: Soak Thoroughly, Then Let Dry

Orchids require careful watering for their foliage and root system to thrive. They should be watered once the potting medium is almost completely dry, typically every 5 to 12 days, depending on the environment and size of the pot they are in. Smaller orchids in smaller pots, such as 2 to 4 inches (5 to 10 cm), will need to be watered more frequently than orchids in larger pots.

Water thoroughly, allowing the excess to drain away, and never let the orchid sit in water. The frequency of watering varies with factors like temperature, humidity and light. You should be letting the potting medium dry out almost completely between waterings. Over-watering can lead to root rot, a common issue with orchids.

One commonly spread myth surrounding orchids is that they prefer to be watered with ice cubes. While this may work for some collectors, I definitely do not recommend watering orchids (or any tropical plant for that matter) with ice cubes! Room temperature, or slightly warmer, water would be a much more suitable option for this tropical bloomer.

Soil: Bark-Based Is Best!

Orchids have unique soil needs compared to typical houseplants. They require a well-draining, airy growing medium, as their roots need equal access to both air and moisture. Orchid-specific potting mixes, often composed of bark, moss and other coarse materials like perlite or charcoal, are ideal. These materials allow for quick drainage and prevent water from accumulating around the roots, which can cause rot.

Regularly check and refresh the potting medium as it can break down over time, reducing its drainage efficiency. The right potting medium is crucial for orchid health, so be sure you aren't just using any ole potting mix.

Temperature and Humidity: Think Tropical Paradise

Orchids generally prefer a warm and humid environment. They do best in temperatures between 60 to 80°F (15 to 26°C), with nighttime temperatures slightly cooler than daytime. Avoid exposing them to temperatures below 50°F (10°C), as cold can be stressful and damaging to orchids.

Orchids also thrive in high humidity, ideally around 40 to 70%. In dry, indoor environments, increase humidity with a humidifier or placing the orchid on or near a pebble tray with water. They will thank you for the extra effort!

Fertilization: Lightly Feed—Less Is More

Orchids benefit from regular but light fertilization to support their growth and flowering. Use a balanced, water-soluble fertilizer formulated specifically for orchids. Dilute the fertilizer to half the recommended strength and apply it every other week during the growing season.

In the dormant period, usually in fall and winter, reduce fertilization to once a month or pause it altogether. Over-fertilizing can harm orchids, so it's important to fertilize them mindfully to provide the necessary nutrients without overwhelming the plant.

Common Problems and Solutions

1. Lack of Blooms: If your orchid isn't blooming, it could be due to insufficient light, incorrect temperatures or improper fertilization. Bright, indirect light is ideal. If natural light is insufficient, consider using grow lights. Orchids often need a difference between day and night temperatures to initiate blooming. Try to provide a cooler environment during the night, ideally a drop of about 10 to 15°F (5.5 to 8°C) from daytime temperatures. This will mimic the plant's natural growing habitat. Fertilize every other week during the growing season and reduce in the dormant period. Be cautious of over-fertilizing, which can harm the plant and inhibit blooming.

2. Wilting Flowers or Buds: Wilting flowers, dried yellow buds or bud drop in orchids can occur due to environmental stress, such as sudden temperature changes or inconsistent watering. Though blooms will naturally fall off with time, you can prolong their existence with the right care. Avoid placing your orchid near air-conditioning vents, heaters or drafty windows. You should also establish a regular watering routine, meaning you will need to observe the growing medium often and determine if the plant needs a drink. Ensuring consistent moisture levels without waterlogging is crucial.

3. Root Rot: Root rot in orchids is often caused by over-watering. Only water your orchid when the growing medium is almost completely dry. This frequency will vary based on factors like light, temperature and humidity but usually ranges from every 5 to 12 days.

If you suspect root rot, carefully remove the orchid from its pot and inspect the roots. Trim away any soft, brown or mushy roots with a sterile instrument, leaving only healthy, firm roots. After removing the affected roots, repot the orchid in fresh orchid potting mix in a clean pot, ideally one that allows for air circulation around the roots, like an orchid basket or a pot with slits.

4. Leaf Spot Disease: Leaf spot disease in orchids typically manifests as small, circular, discolored spots on the leaves, which can be yellow, brown or black. These spots gradually expand and may become sunken or develop a concentric ring pattern. In severe cases, the affected leaves might yellow and drop prematurely. This disease is often exacerbated by high humidity and poor air circulation around the plant.

To treat, start by removing the affected leaves or parts of leaves using a sterilized blade to prevent the spread of the disease. Focus on improving air circulation around the plant; a well-ventilated area can significantly reduce the high humidity that encourages leaf spot diseases. Adjust watering practices to avoid wetting the foliage, as moisture on leaves can promote fungal and bacterial growth. If the infection is severe, you may consider applying a suitable fungicide or bactericide. Follow the product's instructions carefully.

Common Varieties of Orchids

Phalaenopsis Orchid

Phalaenopsis orchids, or moth orchids, are prized for their stunning, mothlike flowers in various colors. Often sold in big box stores, they are arguably the most common variety. These orchids are native to Southeast Asia, with compact sizes and long-lasting blooms.

Psychopsis Orchid

Known as butterfly orchids, psychopsis orchids have unique flowers resembling dancing ladies or butterflies. They come in vibrant colors and bloom for weeks. They are by far my favorite variety of orchid!

Spathoglottis Orchid

Spathoglottis orchids typically feature slender stems with lance-shaped leaves and produce colorful flowers in various shades, such as pink, purple, white or yellow.

Cymbidium Orchid

Often known as boat orchids, cymbidiums are loved for their elegant appearance. These orchids feature long, arching stems with strap-like leaves and produce large, intricate flowers in various colors, including white, pink, green and yellow.

Cattleya Orchid

These orchids possess tall pseudobulbs from which emerge long, leathery leaves and large, fragrant flowers that showcase a wide array of colors, including vivid purples, pinks and whites.

Syngonium

Nature's Arrows

Syngonium, commonly known as the arrowhead plant or arrowhead vine, is a popular houseplant cherished for its graceful, arrow-shaped leaves and ease of care. Originating from the tropical rainforests of Central and South America, this plant's natural habitat stretches from southern Mexico to Brazil, where it thrives by climbing trees and clinging to rocks. Its native environment offers valuable insights into its preferred growing conditions, making it an excellent choice for individuals seeking a touch of the lush rainforest within their indoor spaces.

Syngonium's resilience and adaptability makes it an incredible option for beginners and experts alike. Whether you are a novice indoor gardener or a seasoned green thumb, the syngonium's straightforward care requirements make it a delightful addition to any houseplant collection.

Care Guide

Light: Bright, But Not Blinding

Syngoniums can thrive in a range of lighting conditions, adapting to different levels of brightness. They can do well in settings ranging from bright to medium indirect light, from dappled morning to gentle, ambient sunlight. However, for the most vibrant variegation and lush growth, syngoniums prefer bright, indirect light.

While they can survive in low-light environments, their variegation may be less pronounced and growth may be slower. It's essential to adjust your watering routine in areas with less light, as the plant's slower photosynthesis rate means it requires less water to sustain healthy foliage and growth.

Hello, I am a

Syngonium

 Light: Bright to Medium, Indirect

 Water: Once a Week

 Soil: Rich, Well-Draining

 Toxicity: Not Pet-Friendly

Water: Moisture in Moderation Is Key

These plants require moderate, consistent watering. Check the top 1 inch (2.5 cm) of soil for dryness before watering, allowing it to dry out before giving the syngonium a drink. Once a week during the summer and once every two weeks in the winter would be a good guide to follow, though frequency of watering will always depend on the growing medium. Syngoniums can be prone to root rot, so be sure to not let the soil become waterlogged.

Soil: Rich, Airy and Always Draining

Syngonium plants thrive best in well-draining, nutrient-rich soil. A mix of 45% potting soil and 55% perlite or LECA is ideal, providing both adequate drainage and moisture retention. You can also add compost or worm castings for natural fertilizer. This composition ensures that the roots get sufficient air circulation, preventing root rot while maintaining necessary moisture. Regular soil refreshment or fertilization is beneficial for ongoing nutrient supply.

Temperature and Humidity: Prefers Sauna Conditions

Your home's current conditions are probably just right for syngoniums, as they thrive in temperatures ranging from 60 to 80°F (18 to 26°C).

Although they prefer a more humid environment, syngoniums are adaptable and can do well in the typical humidity levels of most homes. They would, however, appreciate a little extra humidity. Using a humidifier or placing a pebble tray nearby to elevate the moisture in the air would be a welcome treat for them!

Fertilization: Moderate and Balanced

Syngonium plants require moderate fertilization, favoring a balanced, water-soluble fertilizer with an NPK ratio of 10-10-10 or 20-20-20. They benefit from essential nutrients like nitrogen for leaf growth, phosphorus for root health and potassium for overall plant vitality. Fertilize at half strength once a month during the growing season (spring and summer). In fall and winter, if growth slows, reduce to once every 2 months. This routine provides adequate nutrients without over-feeding.

Common Problems and Solutions

1. **Yellowing Leaves:** Yellowing leaves in syngoniums can be due to many issues, with the most common being over-watering. Syngoniums prefer the soil to be somewhat dry between waterings. To resolve over-watering, allow the top 1 inch (2.5 cm) of soil to dry out before watering again and ensure your pot has adequate drainage.

2. **Brown Leaf Tips:** Brown leaf tips in syngoniums are often caused by low humidity. Syngoniums are tropical plants and prefer a humid environment. Increasing humidity around the plant through the use of a humidifier, grouping plants near the syngonium or placing a pebble tray with water under the plant pot can help.

3. **Pests:** Syngonium plants are most prone to spider mites. If you notice them, isolate your syngonium. Hose down your plant with pressurized water. Use an insecticidal soap or neem oil to rid your plant of these bugs. Multiple treatments may be necessary.

A Few Varieties of Syngonium

Syngonium Milk Confetti

Syngonium milk confetti is my favorite variety, known for its arrow-shaped leaves speckled with creamy white or pale pink spots, resembling confetti. This plant is a great choice for pink foliage lovers and beginner plant parents alike.

Syngonium Pink Salmon

This plant features the classic arrow-shaped leaves with a distinctive blend of green and salmon-pink colors. This combination gives it a visually appealing look, making it a popular choice for adding a touch of color to bland spaces.

Syngonium Snow White

The white and green contrast in colors gives this plant a fresh and vibrant appearance, making it a visually appealing addition to any collection. This syngonium is one of the most popular, showing up in almost every big box store and local nursery.

Syngonium White Butterfly

Syngonium white butterfly is known for its foliage that exhibits a pale green to white variegation, resembling the wings of a butterfly. Young plants typically display heart-shaped leaves, but as the plant ages, these leaves evolve into a more complex, lobed or arrow-shaped form.

Syngonium Mojito

This plant is notable for its unique leaf variegation, where each leaf displays a random, marbled mix of green and minty hues. This variegation pattern resembles the muddled lime in a mojito cocktail, hence the name.

Hoya

Waxy Wonders

Native to tropical and subtropical regions of Asia, Australia and the Pacific Islands, hoyas are cherished for their waxy foliage and clusters of star-shaped flowers, often exuding a sweet fragrance. Hoyas are incredibly varied in leaf shape and size, ranging from small and round to large and pointed, with some displaying variegation or unique textures. These plants are unique for their water-storing waxy leaves and flowers that produce a nectar-like secretion, combining drought resilience with a touch of sweet aroma.

Hoyas, often referred to as wax plants, are a diverse and fascinating group of climbing or trailing evergreen perennials. These resilient and adaptable plants are a favorite among many houseplant collectors, valued for their ease of care, long-lasting blooms and ability to thrive in various indoor environments. Their cascading vines make them ideal for hanging baskets or climbing on a trellis. A fun fact about hoyas is that certain stressors like being slightly root-bound, reduced watering and cooler temperatures can encourage them to bloom, especially when balanced with overall plant health and maturity. It took a while for hoyas to grow on me, but these days I am fully obsessed and have officially fallen down the hoya hole!

Care Guide

Light: Lovers of Morning Sun, Avoiders of Afternoon Blaze

Hoyas will thrive in bright, indirect lighting. They can tolerate some direct sunlight, especially in the morning, but too much direct sun can scorch their leaves. A south- or west-facing window that has a sheer curtain is ideal, offering ample indirect lighting.

In lower light conditions, hoyas may grow slowly and produce fewer blooms. Blooms are the most intriguing part about these plants, so you'll want as many as possible! Proper lighting is crucial for encouraging their distinctive star-shaped flowers to bloom.

Hello, I am a

Hoya

 Light: Bright, Indirect

 Water: Every 1–2 Weeks

 Soil: Well-Draining, Chunky Mix

 Toxicity: Pet-Friendly

Water: Enjoys Generous Drinks When Soil Dries

These blooming plants are great for the forgetful plant parent as they prefer their soil to dry out almost completely between waterings. Once the soil is nearly dry, water thoroughly and let the excess drain from the bottom of the pot. You can use a moisture meter or a chopstick to determine the dryness of the soil.

Avoid over-watering to prevent root rot. Watering frequency varies, often every 1 to 2 weeks, but always check the soil first! Slow your watering routine during the winter as the plant will be using less energy during the cooler months.

Soil: Chunky = Happy Hoya

Hoyas require well-draining soil to live a happy and healthy life indoors. A suitable mix often includes a combination of 40% potting soil, 30% perlite and 30% orchid bark. This composition ensures good drainage and aeration, which is crucial for preventing root rot.

Hoyas also benefit from slightly acidic to neutral pH levels in the soil. The inclusion of organic matter, like compost or worm castings, can provide additional nutrients and support healthy growth. It's important to ensure the pot has drainage holes to allow excess water to escape, further safeguarding against over-watering issues such as root rot.

Temperature and Humidity: Cozy Warmth and Moist Air

Hoyas prefer warm and humid conditions. They thrive in temperatures between 60 to 85°F (15 to 29°C) and can suffer if exposed to temperatures below 50°F (10°C) for prolonged periods.

Regarding humidity, they favor a higher level, ideally around 60% or more. This can be achieved through using a humidifier or placing a pebble tray filled with water near or under the plant. Avoid placing hoyas near drafts, heating or air-conditioning vents, as this can disrupt their ideal temperature and humidity levels and might stress them.

Fertilization: Feed Through the Leaves

These tropical plants benefit from a balanced fertilization approach, especially during their growing season (spring and summer). Use a balanced (10-10-10 or 20-20-20 NPK), water-soluble fertilizer. Dilute to half strength and apply it approximately once a month. Including a foliar spray can be beneficial, as hoyas absorb nutrients effectively through their leaves. This is especially helpful for encouraging robust growth and blooming.

Common Problems and Solutions

1. **Lack of Blooms:** Lack of blooms in hoyas is typically due to insufficient light or lack of proper fertilization. Consider moving your plant to a brighter spot, but avoid direct, harsh sunlight, which can scorch the leaves. If natural lighting isn't an option, supplement with grow lights. Use a balanced fertilizer during the growing season to encourage blooms. Over-fertilizing, especially with high nitrogen content, can lead to lush foliage at the expense of flowers. These plants take to foliar feeding very well. Slight stress like being pot-bound or a drop in nighttime temperature can encourage blooming.

2. Stunted Growth: Stunted growth in hoyas can be caused by a number of things, with the most common being insufficient light. Ensure your hoya is placed in a spot where it receives ample, indirect sunlight, or the equivalent with a grow light.

3. Pests: Mealybugs are the most common pests that love to infest our hoyas. To control mealybugs, dab them with a cotton swab soaked in rubbing alcohol. For larger infestations, spray the plant with insecticidal soap or neem oil.

A Few Varieties of Hoya

Hoya Krimson Queen

This hoya's leaves are variegated with creamy white and green colors, often with pinkish hues. The leaves are waxy, oval-shaped and sometimes have a heart-like appearance. The krimson queen is a popular choice for indoor plant enthusiasts due to its wide availability, beautiful variegation and ease of care.

Hoya Kerrii

Commonly known as the sweetheart hoya or valentine hoya, kerrii is a unique, slow-growing plant known for its heart-shaped leaves. Its thick leaves are a vibrant green. The plant often grows as a single leaf cutting, making it a popular gift for Valentine's Day. Unfortunately, some *Hoya kerrii* plants don't grow beyond a single heart-shaped leaf because they are sold without a node, which is essential for producing new stems and leaves.

Hoya Macrophylla

Hoya macrophylla is a beautiful variety loved for its large leaves that feature prominent veins and unique variegation. The leaves are typically green with creamy white or yellow edges and sometimes show splashes of pink. This hoya is known to be very easygoing.

Hoya Bella

Also known as the miniature wax plant, the *Hoya bella* is a charming and petite hoya variety. This plant is particularly admired for its profuse blooms—clusters of tiny, star-shaped, white flowers with pink or purple centers, that exude a subtle, sweet fragrance.

Hoya compacta

Commonly known as the "Hindu rope plant," this plant features unique curled and twisted leaves, making it a visually intriguing addition to any indoor collection. Thriving with infrequent watering, this plant is perfect for those seeking a low-maintenance yet unique house-plant option.

African Violet

Symphony of Velvet Blooms

African violets, or saintpaulia, are known for their colorful blooms and soft, furry leaves. Originating from the cloud forests of Tanzania and Kenya, these plants have adapted very well to indoor environments. They are compact in size, typically growing no more than 6 inches (15 cm) in height, which makes them perfect for small spaces like windowsills or desktops. The African violet's most striking feature is its flowers, which come in a variety of colors including shades of purple, blue, pink and white, often with beautiful patterns and markings.

What sets African violets apart is their ability to bloom multiple times a year with proper care, offering a continuous display of color and beauty. They prefer moderate to bright, indirect light and thrive in consistent indoor temperatures. Their watering needs are unique; they prefer bottom-watering methods to prevent water from settling on their leaves, which can cause damage. With hundreds of varieties available, each with their own unique flower and foliage characteristics, African violets offer endless possibilities for personalization and collection. With nearly 20,000 cultivars to choose from, there is definitely an African violet out there that will speak to you!

Care Guide

Light: Gentle Glow Gets Blooms

These plants require moderate to bright, indirect light to flourish. Ideally, they should receive about 8 to 12 hours of filtered light per day. South- or west-facing windows work well, especially if they are diffused by a sheer curtain. Too much direct sunlight can damage their leaves, causing them to turn yellow or develop scorched spots.

In environments with less natural light, African violets can also thrive under grow lights, which can help supplement their light needs. They will need adequate lighting to bloom, so providing them with a fair amount of UV rays is key to their happiness.

 Light: Bright to Medium, Indirect

 Water: Every 1–2 Weeks

 Soil: Airy, Well-Draining

 Toxicity: Pet-Friendly

Water: Bottom Water, Avoiding Foliage

African violets require consistent, careful watering to thrive. They prefer their soil to be consistently moist, but not water-logged. Over-watering can lead to root rot, while under-watering will cause the leaves to wilt. It's best to allow the top 2 inches (5 cm) of soil to dry out before watering again.

African violets are unique in that they often fare better with bottom watering, where water is absorbed from a tray beneath the pot. This method helps to avoid water settling on the leaves, which can cause unsightly spots. A common myth is that if you get an African violet's leaves wet, it will die. Though this is not true, it is best to spare their leaves moisture.

Soil: Slight Acidity Is Key

African violets require a specific type of soil to thrive, ideally one that is light, fluffy and well-draining. A good African violet potting mix typically consists of 50% potting soil, 25% vermiculite and 25% perlite. This mixture will help to ensure proper aeration and moisture retention.

The soil should be slightly acidic, with a pH around 6.0 to 6.5. It's crucial to avoid heavy, compact soil as it can lead to waterlogging and root rot. Regular repotting with fresh soil every 6 to 12 months can also help to maintain the health and vigor of African violets, providing them with necessary nutrients and preventing soil compaction.

Temperature and Humidity: Cozy Warmth, Gentle Humidity

African violets thrive in temperatures of 65 to 75°F (18 to 24°C) and prefer a humidity level of 40 to 60%. They need to be protected from extreme temperature fluctuations and drafts, so keeping them away from air vents is ideal.

To increase the humidity around the plant, use a humidifier or pebble tray filled with water. You can also group plants together to raise the surrounding humidity levels.

Fertilization: Phosphorus for Flowering

They benefit from regular fertilization to support their blooming and overall health. African violets should be fertilized with a balanced, water-soluble fertilizer formulated specifically for African violets. The ideal ratio is usually 14-12-14 NPK, providing the right balance of nitrogen, phosphorus and potassium. Fertilize every 4 to 6 weeks, diluting the fertilizer to half the recommended strength to avoid over-feeding, which can harm the plant.

During the winter months or when the plant is not actively growing, reduce the frequency of fertilization. This feeding schedule helps maintain vibrant foliage and supports the plant's prolific blooming habit.

Common Problems and Solutions

1. **Powdery Mildew:** Powdery mildew is a common fungal disease that can affect African violets, appearing as a white or gray powdery coating on the leaves. To prevent powdery mildew, ensure your African violets are in a well-ventilated area with good air circulation. Avoid over-watering and water from the bottom to keep leaves dry. Keeping humidity levels moderate is also key. If your plant is affected, isolate it to prevent the disease's spread to other plants. Remove the affected leaves carefully with sterilized pruning shears or scissors. Fungicides specifically designed for powdery mildew can be effective. Be sure to use a product that is safe for African violets and follow the application instructions closely.

2. **Wilting Leaves:** Wilting leaves in African violets are typically a sign of a poor watering routine. To address this, determine if you are over-watering or under-watering. If you are unsure how saturated the soil is, use a moisture meter, wooden skewer or your finger to assess the soil's moisture level. Bottom water when the top 2 inches (5 cm) of soil is dry.

3. **Pests:** African violets can attract many different types of pests with the most common being cyclamen mites. Cyclamen mites are microscopic pests that cause distorted and stunted growth and are particularly challenging to eliminate. Infested plants should be isolated and a miticide can be applied. In severe cases, it would be helpful to invest in predatory mites that will hunt down and eliminate the "bad" mites. Many online stores carry predatory mites and will ship them to your home!

4. **Lack of Blooms:** A lack of blooms can be due to a number of issues, with the most common being insufficient light or improper fertilization. Ensure your African violet is receiving medium to bright, indirect light for most of the day. If natural light is insufficient, consider using a grow light. Use a balanced fertilizer formulated specifically for African violets, with a higher phosphorus ratio, and follow the recommended frequency and dilution.

A Few Varieties of African Violet

Ness' Forever Pink

The Ness' forever pink African violet is a delightful cultivar loved for its vibrant pink flowers that bloom continuously, adding a splash of color and charm to any houseplant collection. With proper care, including bright, indirect light and consistent moisture, this African violet thrives as a stunning and long-lasting addition to home décor .

Irish Flirt

With its dainty white blooms kissed by soft green edges, the Irish flirt African violet exudes charm and elegance. It is a great choice for novice and experienced collectors alike.

Music Box Dancer

Adorned with lovely purple blooms highlighted by white borders, the music box dancer African violet brings a sense of enchantment to indoor spaces. Its moderate light preferences and consistent watering routine make it an effortless addition for plant lovers seeking elegance with ease.

First Kiss Blush

First kiss blush is noted for its blush-pink blossoms and compact growth, making it a wonderful choice for desks and shelves that have bright to medium, indirect light.

High School Sweetheart

The high school sweetheart African violet blooms in shades reminiscent of young love, adding a nostalgic and colorful flair to indoor spaces. The blooms unfurl into a ruffled, unique shape, making it stand out from other varieties.

Tradescantia

Wandering Botanical Charm

Tradescantia, also known as spiderwort or wandering dude, is a versatile and colorful genus of plants that has become a favorite among indoor gardeners. Originating in the Americas, these hardy plants are well-suited to a variety of indoor environments. They are adored for their colorful foliage, which often displays enchanting shades of green, purple, silver and pink. Tradescantia species are widely collected for their ease of care and rapid growth. They are by far the fastest growing plants I have in my collection! I often joke that if you stared long enough, you would be able to literally see the growth forming before your eyes.

What sets tradescantias apart is not just their beauty and fast growth but also their adaptability and resilience. They can thrive in a range of lighting conditions, making them perfect for different home settings. These plants are known for their trailing vines, which look spectacular cascading from hanging baskets or shelves, adding a lush, vibrant touch to any space. Their rapid growth and ease of propagation make them a joy for beginners and a staple for experienced plant enthusiasts. Whether used as a statement piece or part of a diverse collection, tradescantias quickly add a dynamic and colorful element to indoor gardens.

Care Guide

Light: Bright, Indirect for Bright Color

Tradescantias thrive best in bright, indirect light. They can tolerate and adapt to medium light levels, but their distinctive leaf colors and patterns may become less pronounced in lower light conditions. Direct sunlight, especially during the harsh midday hours, should be avoided as it can scorch their leaves. A spot near a window that receives filtered sunlight, such as through sheer curtains, or a position in a room with ample ambient light is ideal. If natural lighting isn't an option, supplement with grow lights.

Hello, I am a

Tradescantia

 Light: Bright to Medium, Indirect

 Water: Every 1–2 Weeks

 Soil: Well-Draining

 Toxicity: Not Pet-Friendly

Water: Moisture Lover, Drought Tolerant

These trailing plants prefer consistent moisture but are also quite forgiving of occasional under-watering. The key is to allow the top 1 inch (2.5 cm) of soil to dry out before watering again, ensuring the plant isn't sitting in waterlogged soil, which can lead to root rot. They thrive in conditions where the soil remains evenly moist but not overly wet.

During the growing season (spring and summer), you may need to water more frequently. In the dormant winter months, watering can be reduced. It's always better to err on the side of slight under-watering rather than over-watering with tradescantias to maintain optimal health.

Soil: Well-Draining Means No Complaining

Tradescantia plants like living in well-draining, nutrient-rich soil. A suitable mix typically includes a blend of 60% potting soil with added 40% perlite or LECA to improve drainage. You can also add in compost or worm castings for a natural fertilizer. This composition ensures that the roots have access to both the moisture and air circulation they need. While they are not overly fussy about soil, maintaining a balance where the soil retains moisture without becoming waterlogged is key to their health.

Temperature and Humidity: Prefers Warm and Humid

Tradescantia plants are quite adaptable in terms of temperature and humidity. They prefer a moderate to warm climate, thriving in temperatures between 60 to 80°F (15 to 26°C). It's important to protect them from extreme temperature fluctuations and avoid placing them near cold drafts or direct heat sources, such as radiators or air-conditioning vents.

While tradescantias can tolerate a range of humidity levels, they do best in moderate to high humidity. If your indoor air is dry, particularly in winter months, consider using a humidifier or placing a water-filled pebble tray beneath or near the plant's container to increase the surrounding humidity.

Fertilization: Half-Strength for Full Color

They benefit from regular fertilization to support their growth, particularly during the spring and summer months. Using a balanced, water-soluble houseplant fertilizer with an equal NPK ratio, such as 10-10-10 or 20-20-20, is recommended. Fertilize approximately once a month but remember to dilute the fertilizer to half the recommended strength to avoid over-fertilizing, which can be detrimental to the plant. In the fall and winter, if the plant's growth naturally slows, reduce feeding.

Common Problems and Solutions

1. **Leggy Growth:** Tradescantia plants need bright, indirect light to maintain compact, bushy growth. Move your plant to a location where it receives more bright, indirect sunlight. This could be near a window with sheer curtains to diffuse direct sunlight. Regular pruning can also encourage more compact growth. By trimming back leggy stems, you stimulate the plant to produce new growth closer to the base, leading to a fuller plant.

2. **Brown Leaf Edges:** Brown leaf edges or tips in tradescantia are often caused by low humidity or inconsistent watering. Ensure the plant is receiving consistent moisture but allow the top 1 inch (2.5 cm) of soil to dry out slightly between waterings. Over-watering or under-watering can lead to stress, manifesting as brown leaf tips. Increasing the

humidity around the plant can also help, especially if your indoor environment is dry. You can do this by placing a humidifier nearby, grouping the plant near other plants or setting the plant on a pebble tray filled with water.

3. Pests: Tradescantia plants, while robust, can occasionally be susceptible to certain pests, with the most common being spider mites. To treat spider mites, first isolate the plant. Use a pressurized water spray to knock off the majority. Spray with an insecticidal soap or neem oil to eradicate the rest. Multiple treatments may be needed to clear the infestation. Increasing the nearby humidity and airflow can help deter these pests in the future.

4. Fading Color: Fading color in tradescantia plants, especially those known for their vibrant leaves, could be caused by inadequate lighting, nutrient deficiency or simply an aged-out leaf. Ensure your tradescantia is placed in an area where it receives bright, indirect light. Consider moving it closer to a window or using sheer curtains to filter direct sunlight. If natural light is insufficient, it's best to supplement with artificial grow lights. Feed your plant with a balanced, water-soluble fertilizer according to the recommended schedule, especially during the growing season. This will help replenish any nutrients the soil may lack and support healthy, vibrant foliage. Lastly, older leaves will die off and lose their color. This is just a part of the plant's natural growing cycle and is completely normal!

A Few Varieties of Tradescantia

Tradescantia Zebrina

Commonly known as the zebrina or wandering dude, *Tradescantia zebrina* is possibly the most popular tradescantia and is known for its striped leaves. The foliage is a deep, shimmering purple with bright silver or greenish stripes, giving it a distinctive zebra pattern. You will find this plant in almost every big box store during growing season!

Tradescantia Nanouk

Tradescantia "nanouk" is known for its robust and fast growth, typically featuring a more upright form compared to other tradescantia species. The leaves are thick, broad and pointed, with colors like pink, green and purple. This unique coloration makes it a popular choice for collectors and my personal favorite.

Tradescantia Spathacea

This plant gets its common name (Moses-in-the-cradle) from the small, boat-shaped bracts that cradle tiny white flowers, reflecting a biblical story. *Tradescantia spathacea* is compact and low maintenance, making it a superb choice for indoor containers.

Tradescantia Albiflora Albovittata

The albiflora leaves are small, lance-shaped and glossy, creating a cascading effect that's perfect for hanging baskets. *Tradescantia albiflora* is a resilient and adaptable species that is extremely easy to propagate!

Tradescantia Sillamontana

This species is known for its compact shape and the contrast between its fuzzy leaves and the occasional bright purple flowers it produces. Its velvety foliage and easygoing nature make it an irresistible plant for collectors.

Dracaena

Tranquil Towers

Dracaena is a diverse genus of plants widely collected for their striking architectural forms and an array of variegated leaves. These easy-to-care-for plants are a staple in the world of interior landscaping featured in many homes, hotels, restaurants, shopping centers, etc. They bring a touch of the tropics to indoor spaces near and far. Originating from various regions in Africa and nearby islands, dracaenas are known for their long, slender leaves and woody stems, which often resemble small trees. Some species grow tall and stately, while others remain compact, making them versatile for different spaces and interior styles.

In addition to their aesthetic appeal and easygoing nature, dracaenas are loved for their air-purifying qualities, making them not just beautiful but also beneficial for indoor environments. They are adaptable to a wide range of indoor conditions, though they prefer bright, indirect light and moderate watering. With their varied shapes, sizes and colors, dracaenas offer something for every level of houseplant collector. Whether you are a novice plant lover or a seasoned collector, you need at least one dracaena in your collection to make it complete!

Care Guide

Light: Prefers Soft Light, Fades in Harsh

Dracaena plants thrive in bright, indirect light but are quite adaptable and can tolerate lower light conditions. They perform best when placed near a window that receives filtered sunlight; avoid the harsh rays of direct afternoon sun, which can scorch their leaves. While they can manage in dimmer areas, their growth may slow and the vibrancy of their leaf coloration might diminish.

For variegated varieties, sufficient light is particularly important to maintain the contrast in their foliage. If natural lighting isn't an option, consider supplementing with a grow light.

Hello, I am a
Dracaena
....

 Light: Bright to Medium, Indirect

 Water: Once Every 2 Weeks

 Soil: Rich, Well-Draining

 Toxicity: Not Pet-Friendly

Water: Even, Light Watering

This genus prefers a consistent watering schedule where the soil is allowed to almost completely dry out between waterings. They are sensitive to over-watering, which can lead to root rot, so it's important to ensure the pot has good drainage and the soil isn't waterlogged.

Water thoroughly until the excess drains out, then wait until the entirety of the soil feels dry to the touch before watering again. Reduce watering frequency in the winter when the plant's growth slows down.

Soil: Let It Drain

Dracaenas require well-draining soil to thrive, as they are prone to root rot if left in waterlogged conditions. A mixture of 40% potting soil, 40% perlite or LECA and 10% orchid bark works well. This mix provides a balance of moisture retention and drainage. The soil should be loose and rich in compost or worm castings to support healthy root growth, natural fertilization and facilitate air circulation.

Temperature and Humidity: Not Too Needy

Dracaena plants prefer a warm and moderately humid environment to thrive. They do best in temperatures between 65 to 75°F (18 to 24°C), which is probably the condition you keep your home in normally. They can tolerate a bit cooler or warmer, but sudden temperature changes or drafts should be avoided.

Dracaenas prefer moderate humidity but can adapt to lower levels typical of indoor environments. If the air is too dry, especially in heated or air-conditioned rooms, the leaf tips may become brown and crispy. Increasing humidity can be achieved through using a humidifier or placing the plant's pot over a tray filled with pebbles and water.

Fertilization: Less Is More

A balanced, water-soluble houseplant fertilizer with an NPK ratio like 10-10-10 or 20-20-20 is ideal. During the active growing months of spring and summer, fertilizing every 6 weeks is sufficient. It is important to dilute the fertilizer to half the recommended strength to prevent over-fertilization and potential salt buildup, which can harm the plant.

Reduce fertilizing in the cooler months of fall and winter if the plant's growth slows down. Since dracaenas are sensitive to fluoride and other chemicals, using filtered or distilled water to mix the fertilizer can help avoid issues like leaf tip burn.

Common Problems and Solutions

1. **Brown Leaf Edges:** Brown leaf edges in dracaena are often due to low humidity. Use a humidifier or place a pebble tray with water beneath the plant to increase humidity around the plant. You can also group it near other plants to create a more humid environment.

2. **Yellowing Leaves:** Yellowing leaves in dracaena can be caused by a number of things, with the most common being over-watering. Allow the majority of the soil to dry out before watering again, and ensure the pot has adequate drainage.

3. **Pests:** Though overall an easy-to-care-for plant, dracaenas can be susceptible to a few different pests—the most common being mealybugs. To control mealybugs, use a cotton swab dipped in rubbing alcohol to remove them, or apply insecticidal soap or neem oil for a large infestation.

A Few Varieties of Dracaena

Snake Plant

Possibly the most common variety, the snake plant is a highly resilient and highly collected houseplant. The leaves are thick, swordlike and can vary in color from dark green with lighter stripes to a silvery-green hue. Snake plants are extremely hardy, tolerating low light and infrequent watering.

Lucky Bamboo

Lucky bamboo is a popular plant often associated with *feng shui* and believed to bring good luck and prosperity. Despite its common name, it's not actually bamboo but a member of the dracaena family. Lucky bamboo is incredibly adaptable and can grow in both water and soil.

Dragon Tree

This beautiful plant features a treelike trunk with a canopy of sword-shaped leaves that are bluish green with reddish edges. Over time, the tree develops a distinctive umbrella-like shape and its trunk becomes more pronounced, resembling that of a small tree. Many people think the dragon tree is a symbol of strength and longevity because it can live for hundreds of years.

Lemon Lime

The lemon lime dracaena (*Dracaena deremensis*) stands out with its striped leaves that feature a mix of green, yellow and lime hues. The leaves are long, narrow and arc gracefully from the central stalk, creating a tropical feel.

Janet Craig

"Janet Craig" is highly valued for its ability to thrive in low-light conditions, making it an excellent choice for indoor spaces that lack abundant natural light. It is a simple yet elegant variety displaying dark green foliage.

Spider Plant

Endless Sprouting Guardian

Spider plants, known botanically as *Chlorophytum comosum*, are one of the most popular and hardy houseplants collected for their lush, arching leaves and ease of care. Characterized by their long, variegated green and white leaves, they bring a vibrant presence to any indoor jungle. Originating from tropical and southern Africa, they are especially noted for their unique reproductive method, producing baby plants or "spiderettes" that dangle from the parent plant like spiders on a web. This is where spider plants get their name.

Spider plants are extremely adaptable and can thrive in a variety of indoor conditions, from bright, indirect light to lower light areas. This, coupled with their minimal care requirements and non-toxic nature, makes them an ideal choice for households, offices and beginners in gardening. Whether displayed in hanging baskets or as a standalone feature, spider plants add a touch of greenery and liveliness to any space. An interesting fact about spider plants is that they are believed to have a mild hallucinogenic effect on felines, which some seem to enjoy! My cats gravitate toward my spider plants over any of my other plants, possibly due to the effects they feel when curiously snipping off a leaf.

Care Guide

Light: Happiest in Bright, Indirect

Spider plants are very adaptable to various lighting conditions, though they thrive in bright, indirect. They can tolerate some direct sunlight, but prolonged exposure to harsh sunlight can scorch their leaves, leading to brown tips or faded coloration. These plants can grow in lower light conditions, although their growth might slow down and the variegation on their leaves may become less pronounced. The ideal placement is near a window with sheer curtains or in a well-lit room where they can receive ample light without the risk of direct sun exposure.

Hello, I am a
Spider Plant

 Light: Bright to Medium, Indirect

 Water: Once a Week

 Soil: Rich, Well-Draining

 Toxicity: Pet-Friendly

Water: Drink Then Dry

These dangling plants prefer evenly moist soil but are quite tolerant of occasional dryness. Water them thoroughly when the top 1 inch (2.5 cm) of the soil feels dry to the touch, allowing excess water to drain away.

During the winter months or in cooler conditions, reduce watering frequency as the plant's growth slows down. Spider plants are forgiving and can bounce back if you occasionally forget to water them, but maintaining a consistent watering schedule will promote healthier growth and prevent the tips of the leaves from browning.

Soil: Nutrient Rich, Well-Draining

Spider plants thrive in well-draining, nutrient-rich soil. A good mix would include a 50% potting soil combined with 50% perlite or LECA to enhance drainage. They prefer slightly acidic to neutral pH levels but are quite adaptable and can tolerate a range of soil conditions.

The key is to ensure that the soil retains moisture while still providing adequate drainage to prevent waterlogging and root rot. Regularly repotting into fresh soil can also help maintain nutrient levels and support the health and growth of your spider plant.

Temperature and Humidity: Comfortable in Moderate Warmth & Moisture

Though adaptable, spider plants prefer temperatures between 65 to 75°F (18 to 24°C), which is typical of most indoor environments. They are somewhat tolerant of temperature fluctuations, but it's important to protect them from extreme cold or heat.

While spider plants prefer moderate humidity, they are not fussy and can tolerate lower humidity levels found in most homes. If the air is particularly dry, especially in heated or air-conditioned rooms, the tips of the leaves may become brown. To increase humidity, you can place a humidifier nearby or set the plant's container on a tray of moist pebbles.

Fertilization: Not-So-Hungry Spiders

Spider plants should be fed occasionally during their active growth period in spring and summer using a balanced (10-10-10 or 20-20-20 NPK), water-soluble houseplant fertilizer diluted to half the recommended strength. Fertilize every 4 to 6 weeks, reducing in fall and winter if the plant's growth slows.

Be cautious of over-fertilization and water quality as spider plants are sensitive to fluoride and other chemicals commonly found in tap water. It is best to use filtered water for these plants to avoid brown leaf tips.

Common Problems and Solutions

1. **Brown Leaf Tips:** This is often a sign of fluoride/chlorine in the water or dry air. Spider plants are sensitive to fluoride, chlorine and other chemicals commonly found in tap water. To remedy this, use filtered, distilled or rainwater for your spider plants to avoid the buildup of fluoride and chlorine. Letting tap water sit out overnight before using can also help some of the chlorine to dissipate. Boost the humidity around your spider plant by placing a humidifier nearby or setting the plant on a pebble tray filled with water. Grouping plants together can also help to create a more humid microclimate.

2. Yellowing Leaves: Yellowing leaves on a spider plant are typically due to over-watering. Make sure you're not over-watering or under-watering your spider plant. Allow the top 1 inch (2.5 cm) of soil to dry out between waterings and ensure the pot has good drainage.

3. Slow Growth: Slow or stunted growth is typically caused by inadequate lighting or nutrient deficiencies. Ensure your spider plant is placed in an area where it receives plenty of bright, indirect sunlight. If natural light is insufficient, consider supplementing with grow lights. Feed your spider plant with a balanced, water-soluble fertilizer during the growing season, following recommended guidelines for dilution and frequency.

A Few Varieties of Spider Plants

Bonnie Spider Plant

The "Bonnie" spider plant, my favorite variety, features distinctive curly green leaves with white variegation. This quirky, easy-to-care-for variant of the classic spider plant produces spiderettes, making it an excellent choice for hanging baskets.

Variegated Spider Plant

Like other spider plants, the variegated spider plant is easy to grow and maintain, thriving in a variety of light conditions and producing baby spiderettes that can easily be propagated. It is a great choice for beginners due to its hardiness.

Bichetii Spider Plant

The Bichetii plant is typically lumped into the spider plant category though it is not a "true" spider plant. It does not produce the popular spiderettes you see stemming from most spider plants, though it does produce white, star-like flowers.

Fire Flash Spider Plant

This plant, scientifically known as *Chlorophytum comosum* "fire flash," is a beautiful variety distinguished by its vibrant green leaves with fiery orange-red margins, adding a burst of color and interest to any houseplant collection.

Green Spider Plant

The green spider plant is a classic variety known for its solid green, arching leaves. Unlike its variegated counterparts, this plant boasts a lush, uniform green color throughout, giving it a more subdued but equally elegant appearance.

Cacti

Tenacious Survivors

Cacti are a widely collected and diverse group of plants, primarily known for their ability to thrive in arid environments. Belonging to the family *Cactaceae*, these plants are distinguished by their thick, fleshy stems that store water, allowing them to survive in some of the harshest conditions on Earth. They come in an astonishing variety of shapes, sizes and colors, from tall, columnar types to round, globular forms. Many cacti come equipped with spines instead of leaves, an adaptation to deter herbivores and reduce water loss.

Native primarily to the Americas, cacti are capable of blooming with colorful flowers that range from small and delicate to large and showy. Their flowering and structural forms make them highly sought after by gardeners and collectors. Cacti are not only celebrated for their striking appearance and resilience but also for their ecological importance and cultural significance. In the home, they are prized as low-maintenance, drought-tolerant plants that add a touch of the desert to indoor settings. They are often recommended for beginners because of their easygoing nature and drought tolerance.

Care Guide

Light: Bright = Blooms

Unlike most houseplants, cacti predominantly require bright, direct light to thrive. They are naturally adapted to the intense sunlight of arid environments and flourish when they can bask in several hours of direct sun each day. For indoor cacti, placing them near a south-facing window where they receive lots of sunlight is ideal.

In general, most cacti can tolerate direct sunlight and even require it to bloom. However, while they are tolerant of high light levels, some cacti may need protection from the harshest midday sun to prevent sunburn. Other species, especially those native to forest understories, prefer partial shade or filtered light to mimic the dappled sunlight of their natural environment. Therefore, it's important to research the specific light requirements for each cactus species to ensure optimal growth.

Hello, I am a

Cactus

 Light: Direct Light

 Water: Every 2–3 Weeks

 Soil: Coarse, Well-Draining

 Toxicity: Not Pet-Friendly

Water: Drench Then Dry

Cacti require deep but infrequent waterings, allowing the soil to completely dry out between drinks. Over-watering can lead to root rot, so it's crucial to ensure adequate drainage while using a well-draining soil mix.

Water more during the active growing season in spring and summer and reduce watering in the fall and winter when many cacti go dormant. These plants can be especially easy to care for because they don't enjoy frequent waterings. Collectors can adopt the "set it and forget it" mindset with cacti.

Soil: Coarse Desert Vibes

Cacti need well-draining, aerated soil with a mix of potting soil, sand and perlite or pumice to prevent water retention and promote root health. They prefer a slightly acidic to neutral pH. Using a cactus-specific potting mix can easily provide the right soil environment to support their growth and reduce the risk of root rot. If you want to make your own mix, I suggest using 40% potting soil, 30% sand and 30% perlite.

Temperature and Humidity: Warm Days, Cool Nights, Low Humidity

Cacti are well-suited to warm and relatively low-humidity environments. They thrive in temperatures ranging from about 70 to 95°F (21 to 35°C) during the day and prefer a slight drop at night. While they can tolerate higher temperatures, they should be protected from extreme heat and frost.

Unlike many popular houseplants, cacti prefer low to moderate humidity, typical of arid and semi-arid regions. In environments with high humidity, ensuring adequate air circulation and soil drainage is crucial to prevent mold and root rot.

Fertilization: Low N, High PK

Cacti have modest fertilization needs compared to most houseplants. Cacti require minimal feeding with a water-soluble, cactus-specific fertilizer, applied once a month during the growing season at half the recommended strength. They prefer a fertilizer with a lower nitrogen content and higher phosphorus and potassium levels, typically represented by an NPK ratio such as 5-10-10 or 2-7-7. Reduce fertilization in the winter if the plant's growth slows. This light feeding regimen supports healthy growth and blooming while preventing the potential harm of over-fertilization.

Common Problems and Solutions

1. **Root Rot:** Root rot is a common and potentially serious problem for cacti, typically resulting from over-watering or poor drainage. At the first sign of root rot (soft, mushy base and foul smell), remove the cactus from its pot and inspect the roots. Cut away any blackened or mushy roots with a sterile knife or scissors. Let the remaining healthy part of the cactus air out and callus over where cuts were made. Repot the cactus in fresh, well-draining soil and a clean pot with adequate drainage holes. Ensure the pot is not excessively large, as this can hold unnecessary moisture. Once repotted, water the cactus sparingly and adjust your future watering schedule to be less frequent, allowing the soil to dry out completely between waterings.

2. **Under-Watering:** Under-watering is a common issue in cacti care, given their association with arid environments and low water needs. However, like all plants, cacti require a certain amount of water to sustain their metabolic functions, even if they are adapted to survive with less. If under-watered, cacti may begin to shrivel or pucker, especially in the

lower or older parts of the plant, as they use up the water reserves in their tissues. They also may look dull in appearance. If under-watering is suspected, start by gradually increasing the watering frequency or amount, ensuring the soil is completely dry between waterings. Avoid the temptation to overcompensate with too much water, which can lead to other issues like root rot.

3. Sunburn: Sunburn in cacti occurs when they are exposed to more sunlight than they can tolerate, leading to damage in their tissues. Sunburned areas may appear bleached, yellow or brown. These patches are typically on the side of the cactus facing the sun. When moving cacti to brighter locations or introducing them outdoors, do so gradually. Increase their sun exposure incrementally over several days or weeks. If a cactus has been sunburned, move it to a spot with less intense light and avoid watering it immediately after the damage is noticed, as the plant needs time to heal. Trim away any severely damaged areas to prevent infection or disease.

4. Nutrient Deficiencies: Nutrient deficiencies in cacti can lead to various growth problems and visual symptoms. Signs of nutrient deficiencies include stunted growth and lack of color. To correct a nutrient deficiency quickly, use a water-soluble fertilizer that contains an NPK ratio such as 5-10-10 or 2-7-7.

A Few Varieties of Cacti

Christmas Cactus

This common cactus typically blooms around the end of the year, near Christmas in the United States, hence its name. With its segmented stems and vibrant blooms in shades of pink, red or white, this plant adds a cheerful and vibrant touch, especially during the holiday season.

Golden Barrel Cactus

Easily found in many big box stores, the golden barrel cactus is noted for its rounded, barrel-like shape and ribbed surface covered in sharp, golden-yellow spines. Native to Mexico, this slow-growing plant can reach impressive sizes. Mature plants may produce a crown of yellow flowers at the top in the summer.

Feather Cactus

Instead of the hard, sharp spines commonly associated with cacti, the feather cactus has clusters of white spines that resemble feathers, giving it a soft and fluffy appearance. This small cactus typically remains compact, making it an ideal choice for indoor containers on windowsills or desks.

Moon Cactus

This popular ornamental plant is loved for its colorful top, which is often grafted onto a green cactus base. The colorful portion, which can be yellow, pink, red or orange, lacks chlorophyll, leading to its bright hue and the plant's common name.

Rat Tail Cactus

The rat tail cactus stems are covered with fine spines and can grow up to several feet in length, making this cactus particularly suited for hanging baskets or elevated planters. The flowers display pink or red hues.

Succulents

Drought-Ready Greenery

Succulents are widely collected plants originating from various arid and semi-arid regions around the world, particularly in Africa, the Americas and parts of Europe and Asia. Known for their remarkable water-storing capacity within their leaves, stems or roots, these plants have adapted to survive even the most forgetful plant parents.

With their unique and often sculptural forms, succulents have become synonymous with modern, low-maintenance plant care. They require minimal watering and are adaptable to a wide range of lighting conditions, making them perfect for both beginner collectors and those with more experience. Their origins in dry, nutrient-poor regions have equipped them with an ability to thrive in similar conditions in homes worldwide. Cacti technically belong in this group because all cacti are succulents, but not all succulents are cacti! Their needs are virtually the exact same with a few exceptions.

From the windowsill to the office desk, succulents offer endless possibilities for transforming a bare space by bringing a piece of their native, exotic landscapes into our personal spaces. Whether you're drawn to the dramatic allure of an aloe or the delicate beauty of a blooming echeveria, succulents provide a durable and delightful addition to any plant collection.

Care Guide

Light: Sun-kissed, Not Sunburned

Succulents thrive in bright light for at least 6 hours daily. While they do enjoy bright, direct lighting, they should be protected from the harshest midday sun to prevent sunburn. Artificial grow lights can supplement natural light, especially in winter.

Rotating succulents ensures even growth and be aware that light affects watering needs—more light leads to more frequent watering. Adjust care seasonally and watch for signs like color changes or stretching to indicate if the light conditions need to be altered.

Hello, I am a
Succulent

 Light: Direct Light

 Water: Every 2–3 Weeks

 Soil: Coarse, Well-Draining

 Toxicity: Not Pet-Friendly

Water: Soak and Dry Method

Succulents require minimal watering, thriving on a "soak and dry" method. Water them thoroughly when the soil is completely dry, then wait until the soil dries out again before the next watering.

Over-watering is a common issue, so ensure good drainage and adjust the watering frequency with changes in light and temperature. In general, less water is needed in cooler or less sunny periods and more in warmer or brighter ones. Always avoid letting water sit in the rosettes of succulents to prevent rot!

A good way to tell if your succulents need water is to observe their leaves. If the leaves look wrinkled or like they are starting to shrivel, they definitely need a drink.

Soil: Happiest in Coarse Soil

Succulents need well-draining soil to prevent root rot, typically a mix specifically designed for cacti and succulents or a combination of potting soil with sand, perlite or pumice. The soil should be porous to allow water to drain quickly and air to reach the roots, promoting healthy growth. Regular potting soil is often too dense and retains moisture for too long, so it's important to use a mix that mimics their natural arid conditions. If you want to make your own mix, I suggest using 40% potting soil, 30% sand and 30% perlite.

Temperature and Humidity: Think Desert Climates

Succulents prefer temperate climates with temperatures ranging from 60 to 80°F (15 to 26°C), typically won't tolerate prolonged frost or extreme heat well. While they can endure higher temperatures if they have adequate airflow and shade, it's vital to avoid drastic temperature changes. During winter, some succulents can go dormant, requiring cooler temperatures and less water.

They thrive in dry conditions with low humidity, mirroring their native arid environments. In very humid environments, ensure good air circulation to prevent mold and rot. Adjust care to mimic their natural seasonal changes for optimal health.

Fertilization: Easy on the Nitrogen

Succulents benefit from a balanced fertilizer with an NPK ratio of a slightly lower nitrogen content, such as 5-10-10. Use this fertilizer diluted to half the recommended strength during the growing season. The balanced mix supports overall health, root development and flowering, without promoting excessive growth that doesn't suit their natural compact form.

As with all fertilization, it's important to apply it during the growing season (spring and summer) and avoid over-fertilizing to prevent root burn and weak, leggy growth. Less fertilization is needed during the slow-growing winter months.

Common Problems and Solutions

1. **Root Rot:** Root rot is typically caused by two main issues: Over-watering and poor drainage. As with cacti (page 137), at the first sign of root rot (soft, mushy base and foul smell), remove the succulent from its pot and inspect the roots. Cut away any blackened or mushy roots with a sterile knife or scissors. Leave the remaining healthy part open to the air to let it callus over where cuts were made. Once callused over, typically within 2 to 3 days, repot your succulent in fresh, well-draining soil and a clean, well-sized pot with adequate drainage holes. Ensure the pot is not excessively large, as this can hold unnecessary moisture. Once repotted, water the succulent sparingly and adjust your future watering schedule to be less frequent, allowing the soil to dry out completely between waterings.

2. Under-Watering: Even though succulents are adapted to survive with minimal water, they still require regular watering to thrive. When you notice signs of under-watering, give the plant a good soak until water runs out of the drainage holes. Ensure the entire root ball gets moistened. After correcting the immediate issue, monitor the plant more closely to establish a more appropriate watering schedule.

3. Sunburn: Sunburn in succulents occurs when they are exposed to more sunlight than they can tolerate, leading to damage in their tissues. Despite being sun-loving plants adapted to bright environments, succulents can still suffer from sunburn. If a succulent has been sunburned, move it to a less intense light and avoid watering it immediately after the damage is noticed, as the plant needs time to heal. Trim away any severely damaged areas to prevent infection or disease.

4. Pests: Succulents can be affected by many different pests, with the most common being spider mites. Treat infestations by first isolating the plant. Spray the plant down with pressurized water. Treat the entire plant, leaves and stems, with an insecticidal soap or neem oil. Multiple treatments may be needed until the infestation is gone.

A Few Varieties of Succulents

Aloe Vera

Aloe vera is probably the most common variety of succulent, widely loved for its medicinal properties. The leaves contain a gel-like substance, known for its soothing, healing properties, especially in treating skin conditions like burns and cuts.

Jade Plant

Jade plants are very popular succulents commonly sold in big box stores and nurseries. They are known for their thick, woody stems and oval-shaped, glossy, green leaves that sometimes have a red tinge on the edges. They are often associated with good luck and prosperity.

Echeveria

Echeveria is a large genus of succulent plants known for their rosette shapes and a wide variety of colors and sizes. Native primarily to Mexico and Central America, these plants feature leaves that can range from green to pink, red, silver and even blue, often with beautiful color gradients and sometimes a waxy or velvety finish. They are extremely low-maintenance, making them a great choice for beginners!

Sempervivum

Also known as hens and chicks, sempervivum is a hardy succulent with tight rosettes of thick, fleshy leaves often colored green, red or purple. These plants are well-known for their ability to propagate through offshoots, forming clusters of "chicks" around the central "hen."

Haworthia

Loved for their distinctive appearance, they typically have thick, fleshy leaves that are green and sometimes translucent, with white bumps, stripes or other markings. Unlike many other succulents, haworthias are generally small, making them perfect for indoor cultivation as houseplants.

Herbs

Flavors of Kitchen Alchemy

Herbs are the quintessential houseplants of the kitchen, infusing culinary creations with fresh flavors and vibrant aromas while adding a touch of greenery to your space. As functional as they are decorative, these versatile plants range from basil and parsley to rosemary and thyme, each with its unique characteristics and flavors.

Growing herbs indoors offers a fresh supply of flavor right at your fingertips, making them a practical and delightful addition to any kitchen. Not only do they elevate your culinary dishes, but they also help purify the air and bring an element of natural beauty to your home. Whether you're a seasoned gardener or a culinary enthusiast looking to dip your toes into houseplant collections, herbs provide a rewarding and aromatic experience, making them perfect for the kitchen.

Care Guide

Light: Bright Light for Best Flavor

Herbs generally thrive in bright conditions and require a good amount of light to grow healthy and provide the best flavor.

Most herbs need about 6 to 8 hours of direct sunlight per day. This is particularly true for Mediterranean herbs like basil, thyme, oregano and rosemary, which are accustomed to sunny, dry climates.

Some herbs, such as parsley, cilantro and mint, can tolerate partial shade, especially in hot climates where the afternoon sun can be too intense. They still prefer bright light but appreciate a break from the midday sun.

When growing herbs indoors, a south-facing window is usually the best spot for ensuring they receive enough light. If natural light is insufficient, consider using a grow light to supplement the necessary hours of light, especially during the winter months.

Hello, I am an

Herb

 Light: Direct Light

 Water: Once a Week

 Soil: Rich, Well-Draining

 Toxicity: Not Pet-Friendly

Water: Delicate Drinks

Herbs prefer consistent moisture but are sensitive to over-watering. They thrive when the soil is allowed to dry out slightly between waterings. Well-draining soil is crucial to prevent root rot.

The frequency of watering depends on the herb type, pot size and environmental conditions, but generally, it's best to water when the top 1 inch (2.5 cm) of soil feels dry to the touch. Some Mediterranean herbs like rosemary and thyme prefer drier conditions, while others like basil may require more frequent watering. Always ensure good drainage in pots to keep herbs healthy and thriving.

Soil: Aerated and Nutrient-Rich

Most of these plants generally need well-draining, nutrient-rich soil. A loose, loamy potting mix works well for herbs grown in containers, providing the right balance of aeration and moisture retention. The soil should allow for quick drainage while holding enough organic matter to nourish the plants.

For herbs like rosemary, thyme and oregano that prefer less fertile conditions, adding sand or perlite can help mimic their native, gritty soils. The ideal pH for most herbs is slightly acidic to neutral (about 6.0 to 7.0). Regularly refreshing or amending the soil ensures your herbs have a healthy foundation for continuous growth and fresh taste.

Temperature and Humidity: Happiest in Typical Household Climate

Herbs generally prefer moderate to warm temperatures, typically between 60 to 70°F (15 to 21°C) but can tolerate a range up to 80°F (26°C) or higher, especially when grown outdoors in the summer. They do not fare well in freezing temperatures and should be protected or brought indoors during cold spells.

Most herbs prefer a moderate humidity level, similar to typical household conditions. However, good air circulation is crucial to prevent fungal diseases, especially in more humid environments. Mediterranean herbs, such as rosemary and thyme, are accustomed to dry conditions and may require lower humidity or more frequent watering to thrive. Adjusting for adequate airflow and avoiding excessive moisture will keep herbs healthy across varying temperature and humidity levels.

Fertilization: Feed Less for Flavor

Herbs generally require moderate fertilization as they can thrive in less fertile soil than many other plants. A balanced, water-soluble fertilizer is suitable for most herbs. Look for something with an even NPK ratio (10-10-10 or 20-20-20) or a formulation specifically designed for herbs.

You should fertilize herbs lightly during their active growing season (spring and summer). Once a month or even less frequently is typically sufficient. Over-fertilizing can lead to lush foliage with diluted flavor, so it's better to err on the side of less. Dilute the fertilizer to half the strength recommended on the package to avoid over-feeding and potential root burn.

Reduce or stop fertilization in the fall and winter when many herbs go dormant or significantly slow down their growth.

Common Problems and Solutions

1. **Over-Watering:** Over-watering is one of the most common issues when growing herbs. To address over-watering, allow the soil to dry, improve drainage and possibly trim affected roots. You can prevent it by checking soil moisture before watering, using well-draining soil and adjusting watering routines to match environmental changes.

2. **Under-Watering:** Under-watering occurs when herbs don't receive enough water to meet their needs, leading to dehydration and stress. To address under-watering, gradually reintroduce water until the soil is thoroughly moistened. Going forward, establish a more consistent watering routine, ensuring the soil stays evenly moist but not waterlogged. Monitor the plant and soil regularly, especially in hot or windy conditions, to maintain adequate moisture levels.

3. **Lack of Light:** Lack of light is one of the worst issues to have while growing herbs as it leads to leggy growth, discolored leaves and lack of flavor. To combat this, move herbs closer to a sunny window or supplement with artificial grow lights, ensuring they receive 6 to 8 hours of light daily. Rotate plants regularly for even growth. Monitoring and adjusting the light exposure based on the plant's appearance and growth patterns can prevent the negative effects of inadequate lighting and promote healthy, flavorful herbs.

4. **Bolting:** Bolting is when a plant prematurely shifts from leaf production to flowering and seeding, often resulting in bitter or less flavorful foliage. Triggered by factors like temperature increases, longer days or stress, bolting is marked by rapid stem elongation and flower development. To prevent or delay bolting, choose resistant varieties, provide a lower level of lighting , ensure consistent watering and harvest regularly. While it's challenging to reverse bolting once it has begun, understanding and managing the triggers can help maintain the quality and longevity of your herbs.

A Few Varieties of Herbs

Rosemary

Rosemary is a fragrant, evergreen herb known for its needle-like leaves and woody aroma. Native to the Mediterranean region, it's widely used in Italian and other Mediterranean cuisines. The plant produces small, blue, pink or white flowers and is valued for its ornamental and culinary uses. Rosemary benefits from regular pruning to encourage bushy growth.

Basil

Basil is by far my favorite herb to use when cooking. Basil plants have a bushy stature, with oval-shaped, vibrant green leaves and can produce small white or purple flowers if allowed to bloom. It is loved not only for its flavorful contribution to dishes like pesto, soups and salads but also for its potential health benefits, including anti-inflammatory and antibacterial properties.

Cilantro

Cilantro is widely used in culinary traditions around the world, including Mexican, Middle Eastern and Asian cuisines. The entire plant is edible, but the fresh leaves and dried seeds are most commonly used in cooking.

Parsley

There are several varieties, including flat-leaf (Italian) parsley, with its more robust flavor, and curly leaf parsley, often used as a decorative garnish. Parsley is also rich in vitamins and minerals, and it's valued not just for its culinary uses but also for its potential health benefits.

Thyme

Thyme is a small perennial shrub known for its aromatic, tiny green leaves and woody stems. It's a staple in culinary, medicinal and ornamental use, originating from the Mediterranean region. Thyme thrives in full sun exposure and needs minimal watering. Thyme comes in several varieties, including common thyme (*Thymus vulgaris*) with its classic flavor, lemon thyme (*Thymus citriodorus*) which has a citrus twist, and creeping thyme (*Thymus serpyllum*), known for its ground-covering ability and floral aroma.

Advanced Care Techniques

Let's dive into the world of advanced care techniques for houseplants, where we focus on the essential skills of pruning, shaping, repotting and propagation. In this chapter, I will explain how to prune effectively for plant health and aesthetics, including techniques like pinching and deadheading. It's important to understand the right time to repot your plants and master a step-by-step approach to ensure their continued vigor. Additionally, we'll explore the rewarding process of propagation, where I'll cover various methods and offer tips for successful rooting and aftercare. By mastering these advanced techniques, you'll enhance the health, beauty and growth of your houseplants, turning your indoor garden into a thriving, vibrant space!

Pruning
and Shaping Your Plants

Pruning is a critical aspect of houseplant care that encourages healthier, more attractive growth. It is more than just the act of snipping away foliage; it is the carefully thought-out removal of growth to enhance your houseplant's overall health and vitality. Pruning involves selectively removing parts of the plant, such as leaves, stems and sometimes even roots in order to: control its shape and size, encourage fuller growth or remove dead or diseased material.

Why Prune?

- **Health:** Removing dead or diseased foliage helps prevent the spread of pests and diseases.

- **Shape:** Pruning helps maintain a compact, aesthetically pleasing shape and can encourage a bushier growth habit.

- **Vigor:** Cutting back a plant can stimulate new growth, leading to a more vigorous plant.

- **Size Control:** Regular pruning can keep a potentially large plant manageable within the confines of your home. This is where root pruning comes into play.

- **Propagation:** Creating multiples of the same plant is possible with your snipped stems or foliage.

When to Prune?

Most houseplants benefit from pruning in the spring or early summer, as this coincides with their active growing season, allowing them to recover quickly. However, I find that pruning even during the cooler months is not entirely off the table, especially if you're in the business of propagation!

If you're looking to shape your plant to make it more aesthetically pleasing—prune in the spring or summer. If you're eager to start growing something new during the fall or winter, there is no harm in taking a cutting to propagate. If your plant has outgrown its pot size but you're wanting to keep it in the same size pot, you can prune off up to a third of the root system regardless of season.

Tools for Pruning

Use sharp, clean pruning shears or scissors to make clean cuts. Clean your tools before and after using to prevent the spread of diseases. I clean my shears with isopropyl alcohol every time I grab them for a chop.

Pruning Techniques

- **Pinching:** Simply use your fingers to pinch off the growing tips of a plant, which encourages the plant to branch out closer to the base.

- **Deadheading:** Snipping off spent flowers will promote more blooms and prevent the plant from wasting energy on seed production.

- **Thinning:** When thinning, you'll be removing some stems entirely, which improves airflow and light penetration throughout the plant. You can propagate these stems if they have a node (the point where a leaf attaches to the stem).

- **Root Chopping:** While not an official term, root chopping is a helpful form of maintenance pruning. You can take up to a third of the root system off of a root-bound plant in order to keep it in the same size pot.

Pruning for Propagation

Remember, many of the cuttings obtained from pruning can be used for propagation. This not only reduces waste but also can increase your collection or provide you with the opportunity to give thoughtful gifts to friends and family. See Propagation Made Easy (page 160) for more on how to turn your singular plant into multiples!

Shaping Your Plants

Shaping is more than just cutting back your plant; it's about envisioning how you want the plant to look and then guiding it in that direction.

How to Shape

- **Directional Pruning:** Prune back stems that are growing in unwanted directions to encourage growth in a more desired form.

- **Staking and Tying:** Use stakes and soft ties to train plants to grow in a particular direction or to provide support for heavy stems. Ties should be fastened loose enough to leave room for the stem to grow but tight enough to hold it in place.

- **Creating Layers:** For multistemmed plants, like dracaenas (page 127), pruning can be used to create a layered look by cutting stems at different heights.

Tips for Successful Pruning and Shaping

- Always prune just above a leaf node, as this is where new growth will typically occur.

- Never remove more than one-third of the plant at any one pruning session to avoid shocking the plant. This goes for foliage and the root system.

- If you're unsure about how a plant will react to pruning, start conservatively. You can always prune more later, but you can't put cut stems back!

- After pruning, care for your plant with appropriate watering and fertilization to support new growth. Be sure your plant is getting adequate lighting so that it bounces back quickly.

Safety First

For plants that have toxic sap, like *dieffenbachia* or *euphorbia*, always wear gloves while pruning and wash your hands afterward.

By incorporating pruning and shaping into your plant care routine, you not only maintain the health and appearance of your houseplants but also get to engage in a creative and rewarding gardening activity. With practice, you'll be able to transform your indoor jungle into a well-manicured collection that reflects your personal style and dedication. And if you're like me, you'll end up with multiples of the same plant all over your home because no pruned stem goes to waste.

Repotting

When and How

Repotting is a crucial component of houseplant care, essential for maintaining vibrant and healthy growth. Knowing when and how to repot will ensure that your plants continue to flourish in your care. This process gives your plants fresh soil, more space to grow and can rejuvenate an ailing or root-bound plant.

If you repot too soon, you run the risk of allowing your root system too much soil and inviting in root rot. If you wait too long, your plant could become stressed to a point that it loses foliage. Let's explore when to repot and review a step-by-step guide on the entire process!

Signs to Look for

Your Plant Might Need Repotting If . . .

Roots Are Growing Through the Drainage Holes: Visible roots poking out of the pot's bottom are a clear indicator it's time for a new home. This is always the easiest way to tell that your plant could go up a few inches in pot size.

Plant Is Top-Heavy and Falls Over Easily: A disproportionate top-to-bottom ratio can mean that the roots have no more room to grow. Carefully pull your top-heavy plant out of the pot to assess the root situation.

Water Runs Straight Through the Pot: Water that zips through the pot indicates that the soil is too compact, or that the plant is too root-bound to retain moisture. If the soil seems to be shrunken down away from the sides of the pot, it is definitely too compact for your plant's liking. Pull the plant out of the pot to observe. If the roots are wrapped about the bottom of the pot or if you see more roots than soil, it is time to upsize pots.

Slowed Growth or No Growth: Even with proper care, if your plant isn't growing, it may need more space to continue its growth cycle. Take into consideration the time of year. If your plant stops growing in winter, it could just be going dormant as plants naturally do. If it stops growing in the warmer months, take a look at the root system to make sure the roots are healthy and have room to spread out.

Visible Salt and Mineral Buildup on the Pot or Soil Surface: This can signal that the soil has degraded and needs replacing. Even if the roots have room to grow, you might consider giving them fresh soil to grow in as this will keep your plant the happiest.

Best Time to Repot

The best time to repot most plants is at the beginning of their active growing season, typically in spring or early summer. This allows the plant to quickly recover and root into the new soil. However, I still find it okay to repot in the cooler months if the root situation needs immediate attention. It is always best to address the issue at hand when you first discover it, no matter the time of year.

How to Repot: A Step-by-Step Guide

1. **Prep Your Area:** Repotting can be messy, so prepping it is an essential step. I like to use my potting mats that snap together on all four corners to create a rectangular work area. These mats have become a staple tool I use nearly every day for many plant-related things. If you don't have a potting mat, definitely look into getting one. You won't regret it!

If you don't have a mat just yet, newspaper or a tarp will suffice. It is also a smart idea to get your vacuum cleaner out (if you are working inside) because messes are inevitable, even with all of the right equipment.

2. **Choose the Right Pot:** The new pot should be about 2 inches (5 cm) larger in diameter than the current one. It is important to ensure it has adequate drainage holes. If the pot you want to use doesn't have drainage holes or is too large for your plant, you can always use a nursery pot and place it in the pot of choice. I do this frequently when I have a decorative planter that I don't want to plant directly in.

When selecting the right pot size for your houseplants, it's important to consider not only the diameter but also the depth of the pot. This is particularly important as different plants have varying root system depths. For example, plants with deeper root systems, such as ficus trees (page 85) or certain palms, require deeper pots to accommodate their extensive roots. On the other hand, shallow-rooted plants like succulents (page 141), African violets (page 117) and most ferns (page 71) thrive in shallower pots. These plants' root systems spread out horizontally rather than deeply, making them well-suited to shallow planters.

3. **Prepare the New Pot:** Make sure your new pot is clean and free of any leftover soil or buildup from previous uses. Place your new pot in your work area and fill the bottom with 2 inches (5 cm) of fresh soil.

4. **Remove the Plant Gently:** It is best to water the plant lightly a day before to make removal easier. Tip the pot on its side and gently ease the plant out. If necessary, push against the sides of the pot to help break it free.

5. **Prune the Roots (if necessary):** You will only need to prune the root system if you plan on using the same size pot as before. Some smaller houses, like mine, can't fit multiple large planters inside of them. If you prune the root system, you will be able to use the same size planter as before while still allowing the plant to grow larger.

To prune the roots, you'll need sharp, clean pruning shears or scissors. Take up to a third of the root system off the bottom of the root ball. If you take more than a third, you could end up shocking your plant, which would cause more trouble than good.

6. Add the Plant to the New Pot: Position the plant in the center of the pot and use fresh potting mix to fill in the area around it. Gently tap the sides of the pot with the palm of your hand to settle the soil and remove air pockets.

7. Water Thoroughly: After repotting, water the plant well to help the soil settle and to reduce transplant shock. You can skip the fertilizer this time around. Fertilizing right after repotting could be too harsh on the freshly repotted root system.

Aftercare: Some houseplant enthusiasts prefer to keep their plant in a shaded area for the first couple of days after repotting to ensure a smooth transition. I find it completely acceptable and even more beneficial to place the plant back in its original spot. Changing up positioning, in my experience, can stress the plant after a repot.

Avoid fertilizing immediately after repotting to prevent burning the roots. You can start fertilizing again once the plant needs another drink, about 1 to 2 weeks after the initial repot and watering. Monitor the plant closely for the first few weeks for signs of stress or transplant shock.

Repotting doesn't have to be an annual event. It's all about observing your plants and responding to their needs. With careful attention and timely action, repotting can invigorate your houseplants, promoting lush, robust growth.

Propagation
Made Easy

Propagating houseplants is more than just a means to increase your collection; it's a deeply rewarding and engaging aspect of plant care. It offers a glimpse into the miraculous processes of plant growth and development. Whether you are looking to fill your living space with more greenery, share plants with friends or simply engage more with your beloved plant babies, propagation is a key skill to master.

This section explores various propagation methods including water, moss, perlite and fluval stratum and provides guidance on creating a propagation box. We'll also delve into the specifics of where to cut the plant for successful rooting.

Water Propagation

Preparation: Let your cutting callus over for 1–24 hours, depending on the thickness of the stem.

Process: Place the cutting in a container of water so that at least one node is submerged. Change the water every few days. Place the container in a well-lit, preferably warm area of your home.

Ideal For: Many tropical plants like pothos, monstera and philodendrons.

Moss Propagation

Preparation: Moisten sphagnum moss and wrap it around the node of your cutting.

Enclosure: Secure the moss with string or plastic wrap to retain moisture.

Maintenance: Keep the moss consistently moist and place the cutting in a warm area with indirect light.

Ideal For: Plants that require higher humidity for root development.

Perlite Propagation

Preparation: Fill a container with perlite and moisten it. Allow the water to slightly pool at the bottom of the container without oversaturating the perlite.

Process: Plant the cutting in the perlite so that the node is buried.

Maintenance: Maintain consistent moisture and place in a location with bright, indirect light. A windowsill that receives warmth from the sun is recommended.

Ideal For: Plants like peperomia or begonias that root easily from stem cuttings.

Fluval Stratum Propagation

Preparation: Fill a container with fluval stratum. Moisten the fluval to where the water is starting to pool at the bottom of the container.

Process: Insert the cutting (or corm), ensuring the node is in contact with the stratum.

Maintenance: Keep the medium moist and provide adequate humidity. You can place a dome on top of the container to ensure adequate humidity.

Ideal For: Aquatic plants, alocasia corms or those benefiting from mineral-rich substrates.

Creating a Propagation Box (Prop Box)

A propagation box, often referred to as a prop box, is essentially a miniature greenhouse created to provide an ideal environment for rooting plant cuttings. It is designed to maintain high humidity and stable temperatures—conditions that are conducive to encouraging root growth in new plant cuttings.

The box usually consists of a transparent or semitransparent container with a lid, which helps to keep the air inside moist and warm. This controlled environment mimics the natural humidity and warmth that many plants require for effective root development, especially those that thrive in tropical conditions.

How to Create a Prop Box

1. **Choose a Container:** Use a clear plastic container with a lid. Storage bins, takeout containers and clear produce containers from the grocery store all work great for prop boxes.

2. **Add Medium:** Fill the bottom with a layer of moistened perlite, sphagnum moss or fluval stratum. You run the risk of rot if your medium is too moist, so be sure it's constantly damp but not soaking wet!

3. **Place Cuttings:** Insert the cut end of the cutting into the growing medium, ensuring the node (or nodes) is buried well. This is crucial because roots will develop from these nodes. Place the cuttings far enough apart to ensure they have ample space for root growth and air circulation. Overcrowding can lead to issues with mold or rot.

4. **Cover:** Close the lid to maintain humidity. Open it occasionally (two to three times per week) and fan your prop box for ventilation.

5. **Location:** Keep the prop box in a warm area with bright, indirect light. Place your box under a grow light for up to 12 hours a day if natural light isn't available. Warmth is key to rooting cuttings in a prop box, so you might need to invest in a seedling heat mat to place underneath.

Tips for Cutting and Aftercare

Cutting Tools: Use sharp, sterilized scissors or pruning shears. To sterilize shears for taking cuttings of houseplants, first clean them to remove any dirt, sap or debris using soapy water. Then, disinfect the blades by wiping them thoroughly with rubbing alcohol (isopropyl alcohol), which is effective in killing most pathogens. Ensure the blades are completely dry before using them on your plants. This process helps prevent the spread of diseases and pests from one plant to another.

Where to Cut: Typically, you should cut just below a node, which is a small bump or swollen area on the stem where leaves, branches or aerial roots grow. The node is the key spot where new roots will develop. For stem cuttings, use a sharp, sterilized pair of scissors or shears and make a clean, angled cut about ¼ inch (6 mm) below the node. This angle increases the surface area for root growth and helps the cutting absorb more water. If propagating a plant like a succulent, choose a healthy leaf and gently twist it off, ensuring it comes away cleanly without tearing. Remember, the precise method can vary depending on the plant species, so it's beneficial to research specific requirements for each type of plant you're propagating.

Leaf nodes are crucial points on a plant's stem from which leaves, and sometimes branches or aerial roots, grow. These nodes are vital for propagation because they contain meristematic tissue, a type of plant tissue consisting of undifferentiated cells capable of rapid cell division. This tissue is what allows the plant to create new growth.

When propagating plants, particularly through stem cuttings, the presence of a leaf node is essential for the successful development of roots. When a cutting with a node is placed in water, moss or another growing medium, the meristematic cells at the node become activated and begin to differentiate into root cells. This process is what turns a simple cutting into a new, independent plant.

Without a node, a stem cutting is unlikely to develop roots and will not grow into a new plant. This is why it's recommended to always include at least one node in any cutting for propagation.

Rooting Hormone: Rooting hormone is a substance used to stimulate root growth in plant cuttings, enhancing their chances of successful propagation. Typically available in powder, gel or liquid form, it contains synthetic auxins, which are plant hormones naturally involved in root development. When a cutting is dipped into rooting hormone and then planted, the hormone encourages quicker and more reliable root formation compared to cuttings without it. This is particularly helpful for plants that are difficult to root or when propagating during less-than-ideal conditions. You can usually find rooting hormone in your local nursery or in the plant section of a home improvement store.

Aftercare: After a propagated plant has developed roots, it is time to transfer it to soil. Start by preparing a pot with well-draining potting mix. Gently remove the rooted cutting from its propagation medium, being careful not to damage the delicate new roots. Make a small hole in the center of the potting mix and place the roots inside, covering them lightly with soil. Water the soil thoroughly, ensuring it's moist but not waterlogged. Place the pot in a location with appropriate light and temperature for the specific plant species.

Initially, keep the soil consistently moist to help the plant adjust to its new environment. Over the following weeks, gradually transition to the plant's regular watering routine. It's also advisable to avoid fertilizing immediately after potting to prevent root burn. With proper care and attention, the newly potted plant will continue to grow and thrive in its new home.

Propagation is both an art and a science. With these techniques, you can effectively turn one plant into many. Remember, each plant species may have specific needs, so always research your plant for the best propagation method.

DIY Plant Projects

Who doesn't love a good DIY project that blends houseplants and creativity? This chapter offers a range of engaging and enjoyable activities that go beyond traditional plant care, focusing on adding a unique and personal flair to your indoor jungle. These projects are not just about beautifying spaces; they're about exploring new skills, expressing artistic talent and enhancing the relationship you have with your plants.

Whether a seasoned crafter or new to the DIY scene, these projects provide a fulfilling way to connect with nature. From creating space-saving designs to crafting one-of-a-kind plant displays, each activity marries practicality with aesthetic charm. Tackle one of these projects by yourself on a rainy day or with friends and family for a fun group activity!

Self-Sustainable Terrarium

Creating your own miniature ecosystem might sound complicated; however, it is much simpler than you might anticipate! A self-sustaining terrarium is not just a vibrant, aesthetically pleasing addition to your space, but a satisfying exploration into the intricate balance of nature itself. Within the glass walls of a terrarium, life endlessly unfolds, offering a front row seat to the cycles of growth, decay and rebirth.

This step-by-step project will guide you in crafting a living, breathing biome that requires minimal intervention. Creating the terrarium itself can be thought of as a form of meditation, while watching the timeless dance of life afterward leaves you feeling forever satisfied with your completed project.

Choosing your vessel: You'll want to consider a few things when choosing the right vessel for your terrarium: transparency, size and shape, closure and aesthetic.

Opt for a clear, non-reactive glass to ensure unobstructed viewing and ample light for photosynthesis. A spacious vessel that allows room for growth will be best in the long run. Be sure to consider how wide the opening is for easy assembly. You will want a vessel that fully seals for it to be a true, self-sustaining terrarium. Choose a vessel with a lid that fully seals the enclosure but is removable for occasional airflow. Lastly, choose a vessel that not only fits the above description but also matches your home's aesthetic. This terrarium will be part of your indoor jungle forever, so you'll want something that is timeless and matches your personality!

Choosing your plants: Selecting a plant for a self-sustaining terrarium involves considering the specific environment inside the enclosure and matching it with plants that will thrive in those conditions. Key factors include choosing plants that prefer high humidity and indirect light, and ensuring they are small enough to fit comfortably within the terrarium without outgrowing it quickly. Varieties like mosses, nerve plants and peperomia are often popular choices; I used a ruby red nerve plant in this example. Steer clear of plants like succulents or cacti. If you plan on adding multiple plants, consider plants that have similar care needs to create a harmonious, low-maintenance ecosystem where each element supports the others.

You will need . . .

- LECA or small pebbles
- 1 glass vessel with closure
- Cheesecloth (cut to the shape of the base of your vessel)
- Dried sphagnum moss
- Activated charcoal
- Potting soil
- Wooden skewer, chopstick or long tweezers
- Houseplant(s) of choice
- Spray bottle
- Water

Step 1: Rinse off your LECA or pebbles and add them to the bottom of your terrarium. At least a 1-inch (2.5-cm) layer will be needed, but you can add more depending on the size of your vessel. This will be your first layer for draining purposes.

Step 2: Place your cheesecloth over the LECA or pebbles. If it doesn't fit perfectly, that is fine! You can tuck the sides down and around the bottom drainage layer if you wish. This is to prevent any of the next layers from falling into your drainage layer.

Step 3: Add 1 to 2 inches (2.5 to 5 cm) of dried sphagnum moss. Rip your moss apart so that there aren't any large chunks. Sphagnum moss helps with drainage and water retention.

Step 4: Add ½ to 1 inch (1.3 to 2.5 cm) of activated charcoal on top of the dried moss. Activated charcoal will absorb any sitting water while also preventing odor and bacteria buildup.

Step 5: Add at least 1 inch (2.5 cm) of potting soil over the activated charcoal. You can add more depending on the size of your vessel.

Step 6 (Optional): If using live moss, now is the time to place this where you'll want it to take hold on top of the potting soil.

Step 7: Create a small hole where you want to place your plant using a wooden skewer, chopstick or long tweezers. Place your plant in the hole and use your tool (or fingers) to position the soil back around the base of the plant to secure it in place.

Step 8: Almost done! Time to add your water. Using a spray bottle is best for this. As you spray your terrarium, you will see the water pooling at the bottom of the drainage layer. Once there is a very thin layer of water at the bottom (about one-fourth of the way up the drainage layer) you'll know that you have added enough water.

Step 9: Secure the lid on the top of your terrarium and place it in a well-lit area of your home. North-facing windows work extremely well as they provide a consistent, indirect light, which will be perfect for most terrarium plants. You can also use a grow light if natural lighting is not available.

Aftercare: *It is best to air out your terrarium once a week. Do this by taking the lid off for 10 minutes and securing it back on afterward. Trim your plants and moss growth back as needed. It is best to leave the trimmed cuttings in the jar as they will act as a natural fertilizer for your living plants! It is time to water your terrarium once the drainage starts drying out, or about once every 3 to 4 months.*

Living Wall

A living wall with houseplants can transform an indoor space into a lush, green oasis. In the midst of the pandemic, I came up with this super simple yet delightfully pleasing living wall concept that anyone can replicate. Creating a living wall with houseplants is not just about adding greenery to your environment; it's about bringing a piece of nature into your everyday living space, enhancing both the aesthetics and the air quality of your home. Living, breathing wall décor is an incredible way to enhance any space and create a talking point among guests! The following DIY guide will walk you through setting up a living art installation using six pots that hook onto two dowels mounted on the wall. It's an easy yet striking way to display your plants in your home!

Choosing your plants: Almost any plant can be a part of your living wall, though for the best success, pick plants that share similar lighting requirements. For this project, I chose to pair pothos, philodendron and ivy. As you pick your houseplants, keep in mind the amount of light your wall location receives. If natural lighting isn't available, consider installing a grow light above the living wall.

You will need. . .

- 2 wooden dowels (length depending on wall space)
- Optional: paint or wood stain for the dowels
- Tape measure
- Level
- Pencil
- Drill and screws (appropriate for your wall type)
- 4 wall brackets or eye hooks for dowels
- 6 wall-mounted plant pots with hook attachments
- Potting soil
- Houseplants of your choice

Step 1 (Optional): If desired, paint or stain the wooden dowels to match your décor. Let them dry completely.

Step 2: Decide on the horizontal arrangement of the dowels on your wall. They should be spaced apart according to the height of the pots to ensure each plant has enough room to grow.

Use a tape measure and pencil to mark the positions accurately and a level to ensure the dowels will be straight.

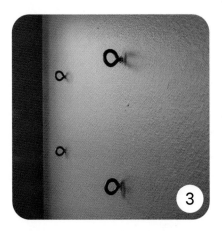

Step 3: Install two brackets or hooks for each dowel on the wall. Use a drill to make pilot holes, then screw the brackets or hooks securely into the wall. Make sure they are sturdy enough to hold the weight of the dowels with pots and plants.

Step 4: Place each dowel onto its corresponding brackets or hooks.

Step 5: If the pots aren't already equipped with drainage holes, drill some small holes to prevent waterlogging. Fill each pot with potting soil and plant your chosen houseplants.

Step 6: Hook the pots onto the dowels. Ensure they are securely attached and balanced.

Step 7: Step back and look at your living wall. Adjust the positioning of the pots, if necessary. If one side of the living wall receives more light than another, adjust the order of the pots according to individual plant needs.

Aftercare: Top water (page 20) the plants as needed, based on their individual care requirements. Be mindful of water dripping onto the floor or furniture below and consider using a protective tray or cloth if necessary. I enjoy using catch trays that hook onto the pot to catch excess water. These trays can be added when you plan to water and removed once finished.

Regularly tend to your plants, prune when necessary and enjoy the dynamic touch of nature they bring to your indoor space.

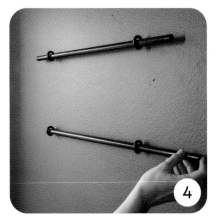

Self-Watering Vases

This self-watering vase DIY is one of my favorite, most aesthetically pleasing plant projects to date that requires supplies you might already have on hand. Not only does it act as a helpful tool for the sometimes forgetful plant parent, it also resembles a type of "plant parfait" that will be a hot topic of conversation among your house guests. You can expect to witness your plant's roots weaving their way through the vessel, only adding to the unique appearance of this project. These vases make incredibly interesting centerpieces on tables that receive adequate lighting, or thoughtful gifts to plant lovers in your circle.

Choosing your vessel: It all begins with your vase of choice. Things to consider when choosing the right vessel are transparency, size and shape and aesthetic. I typically reach for a clear, non-reactive glass vase when creating these pots, though you can get away with a semitransparent vessel as sunlight does not need to pass through the vessel. Some transparency is necessary in order to see how thick your layers are and to observe the water line.

Your plant will be reaching through the top of the vase's mouth, so it should be wide enough to accommodate the stems and leaves with some room for growth. The mouth width of your vase will need to be 2 to 4 inches (5 to 10 cm) wider than the size of your plant's root system. The vase can be as tall as you wish—the taller, the better. If your vase is tall, it will retain more water, which will require less maintenance on your end. Choose a vase with a wide mouth so that it is easier to build.

An equally important feature is the aesthetic your vase provides. Thrifting is a great option if you don't have a vase that speaks to you already at home!

Choosing your plant: The plant you choose will need to be okay with slightly moist conditions 24/7. I have had success with alocasias, philodendrons, pothos and monsteras in this DIY setup (I used a Thai constellation monstera for this project in particular). Other types I would have confidence in would be ferns, peperomias, calatheas, marantas, syngoniums and a few varieties of herbs.

You will need. . .

- 1 synthetic, nylon rope (You will be placing the rope in the vase with both ends hanging over opposite edges. For a typical-sized flower vase, you will need 6 inches [15 cm] of rope hanging over both sides, so allow enough rope to ensure this is the case. More rope is better than less.)
- 1 transparent or semitransparent vase
- LECA
- Dried sphagnum moss
- Potting soil
- Houseplant of choice
- Water

Step 1: Find the middle point of your rope by folding it in half and lining up the two ends. Place your rope in the vase with the midpoint in the center of the bottom. Allow 6+ inches (15+ cm) of rope to hang over both sides of the vase. This will act as your water wick.

Step 2: While holding your rope in place, pour the LECA into the vase. You will need at least 2 inches (5 cm), but you can use more depending on the size of your vase. The more you add, the less frequently you will need to add water.

Step 3: Add 1 to 2 inches (2.5 to 5 cm) of dried sphagnum moss on top of the LECA. This will act as your barrier between the potting soil and the drainage layer.

Step 4: Add 2+ inches (5+ cm) of potting soil, depending on the height of your vase, on top of the sphagnum moss.

Step 5: Place your plant of choice in the center of the vase.

Step 6: Add another 1 to 2 inches (2.5 to 5 cm) of soil, halfway covering the root system. Wrap the excess rope around the middle of the plant's root system. Don't wrap too tightly or loosely. There is a happy medium that is easy to find. Your rope will wick the water from your drainage layer and provide your plant with slow but consistent moisture.

Step 7: Add potting soil until you have reached the bottom of your plant's stems and foliage.

Step 8: Time to water! Saturate the soil with water and watch it pool at the bottom of the LECA. It is best to allow water to fill two-thirds of the way up the LECA. No fertilizer will be needed for the first round of watering.

Step 9: Place your self-watering vase in an area that receives adequate light for your plant of choice. If you don't have an area that receives proper natural lighting, supplement with a grow light.

Aftercare: *This easy DIY doesn't require much aftercare or upkeep, which is why it's one of my favorites. You will need to water with added liquid fertilizer from here on out. I always like to keep the water line two-thirds of the way up the LECA. You can expect to water about one to two times a month depending on the size of your vase and the height of your drainage layer.*

The roots of your plant will start growing into the moss and LECA layers. This is totally normal and nothing to worry about. They will adapt as they move from layer to layer.

You'll know it's time to repot your plant when the roots start wrapping around the bottom of the vase. You can either repot into a larger vase with this same process or pot it directly into a potting mix. The choice is yours!

Lamp Shade Plant Stand

If you love thrifting "one man's trash" as much as I do, then you're going to love this lamp shade upcycle. You can turn practically any lamp shade into a chic, modern-looking plant stand in just a few simple steps. Gone are the days of overpriced plant stands that never seem to be the perfect height!

Choosing your lamp shade: When choosing the perfect lamp shade to use for a plant stand, you'll want to think about where it will be placed in your house and what size plant pot you'll be placing in it. If it will be placed on the floor, you're likely going to want it to be pretty tall. If it will be residing on a desk, you could opt for a mini lamp shade. Taking a measurement of the height you're looking for as well as the plant pot size before you go thrifting is always a smart idea!

If you're upcycling a shade that you already own, find somewhere to place it that will receive an adequate amount of light for your plant of choice. If natural light isn't an option, supplement with a grow light.

Choosing your paint: Select a color that will match the décor around the area you plan on placing your stand. This choice is completely up to you. Bright and bold or soft and muted? Gloss finish or matte finish? Quick dry or overnight? If you're like me and have little patience when it comes to fun DIY projects, you might want to choose a paint with a shorter dry time.

You will need. . .

- 1 lamp shade with circular top
- Scissors
- Wire cutters
- Spray paint (any color, any finish)

Step 1: Cut any fabric off of your lamp shade using scissors.

Step 2: Typically, there will be four wires you need to snip off at the top of the shade to open the circular ring completely. If so, place your wire cutters as close as possible to the outer top ring and snip off all four attached wires. You might be snipping more or less depending on the style of your lamp. If there are no wires blocking the hole, you can skip this step.

Step 3 (Optional): Take your lamp shade to an area that you can safely spray paint it to your color of choice. I use a bed sheet that I have dedicated to crafting and lay it out in my yard. Spray paint the entire stand and let it dry for the amount of time directed on the can.

Step 4: Place the stand in your desired location and situate your plant on top. You may find yourself simply placing the pot on top of the ring or the ring might allow the pot to be placed inside of it, catching at some point.

Creating a *Kokedama*

A *kokedama*, which translates to "moss ball" in Japanese, is a beautiful and unique way to display your houseplants. This style of Japanese garden art transforms plants into a sculptural element by wrapping their roots in a ball of soil and moss, then securing it with string. Here's a step-by-step guide to creating your own *kokedama* using potting soil, clear string and sheet moss.

Choosing your plant: Almost any plant will adapt and grow in a kokedama, but my favorite plants to use are pothos, ivy, syngonium and small ferns. I used a syngonium pink salmon for the kokedama pictured.

You will need. . .

- Houseplant of your choice
- Potting soil
- Water
- Sheet moss (live or preserved)
- Clear string
- Scissors
- Gloves (optional)

Step 1: Choose and prep a small houseplant. Remove it from its pot and gently shake off excess soil from the roots, being careful not to damage them.

Step 2: Mix your potting soil with water until it's moldable but not overly wet. You're aiming for a consistency that holds together without dripping water.

Step 3: Take a portion of the soil mixture and form it into a ball around the plant's roots. The size of the ball will depend on the size of the plant but should be large enough to accommodate all the roots.

Step 4: Soak your sheet moss in water for a few minutes until it's pliable. Wring out any excess water.

Step 5: Lay out the sheet moss and place the soil ball in the center. Wrap the moss around the soil ball, covering it completely.

Step 6: Take the clear string and start wrapping it around the moss ball to hold everything in place. Wrap the string tightly enough to secure the moss to the soil ball, but be careful not to compress it too much. Crisscross the string in various directions for a secure hold. Tie off the ends and cut off any excess string.

Step 7: Trim any stray moss to give your kokedama a neat, rounded appearance.

Step 8: To water, soak the entire moss ball in water until it's fully saturated (about 10 minutes), then allow it to drain before hanging or placing it back in its display spot. Skip the liquid fertilizer for the first watering. Afterward, it is in your best interest to add liquid fertilizer to the water you soak your kokedama in so that it receives vital nutrients.

Aftercare: *Place your kokedama on a decorative tray or dish. Ensure it's located in a spot with appropriate light and temperature for the type of plant you've chosen. Keep in mind the more light that you provide, the quicker your kokedama will dry out.*

Your kokedama watering needs will vary, but typically you will need to water one to two times per week depending on the size. Pick up your kokedama and feel the weight; if it's light, it probably needs a drink.

It's time to upsize your moss ball or repot into a planter when you start noticing roots poking through the outer layer of moss. When upsizing, unwrap the clear string around the ball. Apply more soil to the outer layer around the moss and cover with sheet moss again, securing with more of the clear string. If potting into a planter, unwrap the string and place the entire ball into a planter 2 inches (5 cm) larger than the ball. Fill with potting soil and water as needed.

Creating a kokedama is a rewarding, hands-on way to engage with your plants and add a touch of natural art to your home. Each one is unique, and with care, your kokedama can be a long-lasting and beautiful living display.

Continuing Education and Resources

As we venture to the end of this book, it is important to remember that caring for houseplants is a continuous journey of learning and growth, much like the plants themselves. Each leaf, stem and flower in your home offers a living lesson in patience, care and adaptability. Whether you're a seasoned green thumb or a budding plant enthusiast, there's always more to discover and enjoy in the world of houseplants!

Embrace Experimentation

Your home is a unique environment, and each plant has its own set of needs and preferences. Don't be afraid to experiment with different plants, placements and care techniques. Remember, occasional setbacks like a wilted leaf or a pest invasion are opportunities to learn and grow. These are never signs of improper plant care, just another teachable moment. Trial and error is the best way to go about this hobby.

Stay Curious

The world of houseplants is vast and varied. Stay curious and open to new information. Subscribe to gardening blogs, join local plant societies or follow online communities dedicated to houseplant care. YouTube has been a great resource for me! Books and magazines can also be a treasure trove of advanced techniques and inspiring garden stories. Staying curious and excited to learn is the best thing you can do for your indoor jungle.

Continued Education

Enroll in workshops or courses offered by local botanical gardens, nurseries or community colleges. These can provide hands-on experience and deeper insights into specific aspects of plant care, such as propagation, pest management or landscape design. You can also learn an incredible amount from seasoned collectors, whether they be online or in person.

Attend Shows and Expos

Plant and garden shows are fantastic places to see a wide variety of plants, learn from experts and meet other plant lovers. They can also be a great source for finding rare or special varieties to add to your collection or to your wish list. You will quickly fit right into the crowd!

Leverage Technology

Utilize apps and online tools for plant identification, care reminders and community advice. These can help you diagnose problems, keep track of watering and fertilization schedules and connect with other enthusiasts for tips and support. There are many apps available for download that prioritize specialized care techniques and community.

Share Your Passion

Share your experiences and knowledge with others. Whether it's through social media, blogging or simply chatting with friends and family, spreading the joy of plant care can be deeply rewarding. I have converted many of my friends and family members into "plant people" simply by chatting about how much this hobby has transformed my life! Plus, teaching others is a great way to reinforce your own knowledge.

Reflect and Adapt

Take time to observe your plants and reflect on their growth. What worked well? What might you change? Adapt your care routine as you learn more about each plant's needs and as they grow and change through the seasons. Again, trial and error is the best course of action for learning and growing in this hobby.

Your journey with houseplants is a personal one, filled with growth, learning and the joy of nurturing living things. As you continue on this path, remember that resources are plentiful, and the plant community is always here to support you. May your home be ever green and your heart ever joyful in this lifelong journey with your leafy friends. Happy growing!

Acknowledgments

As I reflect on the journey that writing this book has been, I am deeply grateful for the support and encouragement I've received from many. This book would not have been possible without the collective wisdom, support and patience of the following:

First, I would like to thank my family. To my husband, Dalton, who has been an endless supply of love and support throughout this journey and to my mom, Michelle, who has always pushed me to follow my dreams. My accomplishments would not have been possible without both of your support and love.

A huge thank you to Matkins Greenhouse and Garden City Nursery in Bentonville, Arkansas for allowing me to visit and photograph some of their beautiful plants for this book.

I also owe a tremendous thanks to everyone at Page Street Publishing Co. for believing in my vision and helping me see this book to fruition. I truly appreciate the support and advice I have received from everyone at Page Street.

Lastly, I want to thank you, the reader, for embarking on this green journey with me. Your curiosity and passion for learning are what ultimately bring this book to life. I hope it serves you well.

With deepest gratitude,

Kellyn Kennerly

About the Author

Kellyn Kennerly is a houseplant enthusiast with over five years of experience in gardening and caring for common and rare varieties of houseplants. After years of hands-on experience, research and learning from trial and error, she has dedicated a majority of her time to helping others curate their houseplant collection while also giving them the tools to keep it thriving. Kellyn has quickly risen past half a million followers on social media and her numbers continue to grow as she posts short-form video content about plant care topics.

Beyond her professional life, Kellyn is passionate about gardening, staying active, living sustainably and helping others. She wrote *Happy, Healthy Houseplants* to ensure that everyone has the basic tools and knowledge to keep their personal plant collection thriving for years to come. Currently, she is continuing to create free videos and upload them across Instagram, Facebook, TikTok and YouTube to help spread care tips and enthusiasm about houseplants across the world, always seeking to explore and understand the botanical world more deeply.

Kellyn lives in Northwest Arkansas with her husband, two dogs, two cats, three chickens and leopard gecko. When not writing or creating video content, she enjoys cooking, traveling with her husband, working out and enjoying the simple things in life.

To learn more about Kellyn Kennerly or to get in touch, follow her on Instagram @easygrowing_ or visit www.easygrowing.shop.

Image Credits

Index